Praise

"Like the sun's sacred vows [...] fe, so too should each heart love [...] ok by Janet Conner help unfurl t[...] ...any. May blessed words, as they can, complete us. Discovering the Presence that makes the atoms dance will reveal our own astounding beauty and a wild, holy, majestic giving like the mountains and the sky." —**Daniel Ladinsky,** international bestselling Penguin author

"In *Soul Vows,* Janet Conner has provided seekers with a sure, rich and deeply fulfilling path to spiritual advancement and genuine knowingness. It is one thing to hold a theoretical sense of the Divine, and quite another to open to immersion in the Indwelling Beloved. I invite you to feast upon and savor the wisdom and practices within this powerful book, for you will be lavishing yourself in the exquisite possibilities of your True Nature!" —**Dr. Roger Teel,** senior minister, Mile Hi Church, author of *This Life Is Joy*

"Open this book if you have been in the shallows longing for the deep. Janet will guide your way to more of your divine self, shining as the light of the world." —**Linda Martella-Whitsett,** author of *How to Pray Without Talking to God* and *Divine Audacity*

"This profound but practice-based book is a joy to recommend! It surely represents a new and needed wave in spiritual teaching, where teachers like Janet Conner are not afraid to speak of divine intimacy— yet in a way that is far beyond mere sentiment—and which invites the reader to actual experience. Water is good, but Janet changes it into intoxicating wine." —**Richard Rohr,** OFM, Center for Action and Contemplation, author of *Falling Upward* and *Immortal Diamond*

"Janet Conner is a spiritual teacher for the 21st century: part guru, part girlfriend, a writer able to translate deep truths into practical action. In *Soul Vows,* she awakens the mystic in each of us and gently prods us to make good on the silent promises from deep within." — **Victoria Moran,** author of *Creating a Charmed Life* and *Shelter for the Spirit*

"*Soul Vows* is Janet Conner's best book yet! Prepare for a deep dive into your Self." —**Ellen Debenport,** author of *The Five Principles* and *Hell in the Hallway*

"This is a wonderful book, gracefully and wisely written. Anyone on a spiritual path will learn a great deal from it." —**Andrew Harvey,** author of *The Hope: A Guide to Sacred Activism*

"Janet Conner's *Soul Vows* teachings have been a gateway to my mystical self, an initiation to a sacred journey of feeling grounded in the Earth while connected to the Divine. This book takes you on a life-changing escapade of finding your inner truths and powerfully infusing yourself with them daily. Janet is an extraordinary storyteller and spiritual teacher. She masters the complex and then gives you her synthesis and the specific keys to the Kingdom. Opening this book is like lifting the lid on an ancient Treasure Chest, full of sacred secrets and invitations. My gratitude to Janet; her wisdom is infinite." —**Gail McMeekin,** author of *The 12 Secrets of Highly Creative Women* and *The 12 Secrets of Highly Successful Women*

"Janet Conner has written a beautiful-yet-practical book that is no less than a map to discover our mystical heart. In *Soul Vows,* she illuminates the way, step by step, so that we can learn to listen and trust our own still small voice, guiding us to our deepest union with Life. Read this book and you will discover the path that leads to the Divine within." —**Joel Fotinos,** author of *My Life Contract*

"Do you hear that unanswered longing calling from your soul? Janet Conner guides you in the process of giving answer to that call with profound skill. In this work Janet draws upon many disciplines and sources, as well her own deep processes. I predict *Soul Vows* becomes your companion in finding your own finest answers to your spiritual longing." —**Mary Anne Radmacher,** author of several books including *Lean Forward into Your Life* and *Live with Intention*

"Janet Conner's *Soul Vows* is a mirror reflecting the Presence that is you. You don't so much read this book as peer into it and allow it to show you what you already know and who you already are. You won't be disappointed." —**Rabbi Rami Shapiro,** author of *Perennial Wisdom for the Spiritually Independent*

"In *Soul Vows* Janet Conner issues a clear invitation to each of us to wake up to the sacred agreement we've each made with our divine Source. And when we wake up not only do we activate our deep connection with the Divine, we also come to know who we are, what we are here to do, and to live our lives with a grace that feeds our heart and nourishes our soul." —**Susyn Reeve,** author of *The Whole-hearted Life* and *The Inspired Life*

"With elegant, graceful, poetic prose, Janet Conner shows herself again to be one of our most gifted spiritual writers. This book is like the song of the soul. The greatest insight this book offers is the realization that we—all of us—come from Love and . . . ultimately . . . return to Love. There is no other origin . . . no other destination . . . no other place to be." —**Ramananda John E. Welshons,** author of *One Soul, One Love, One Heart*

"My favorite part of this book is its celebration of paradox. With her succulent writing, joyful spirit, and refreshing vulnerability, Janet Conner expertly guides us into a sacred relationship with all that is. She is not prescribing easy answers; she is inviting us into the living mystery, which is love, which is, as it turns out, who we really are." —**Mirabai Starr,** translator of Teresa of Avila, John of the Cross, and Julian of Norwich, author of *God of Love: A Guide to the Heart of Judaism, Christianity & Islam*

"As we experience the heartfelt steps of questioning, writing, listening, chanting, and moving, we find ourselves climbing to higher states of awareness... right along with the paradox of going deeper and deeper into the mystery of who we are with each revelation.

"Through the seven chakras, Janet Conner beautifully illustrates how everyone is wired to experience the Divine directly. As each vow from our soul is uniquely discovered in each chakra, we finally find our most natural personal statements until we feel whole and our soul vows feel complete. We ultimately become comfortable expressing the magnificent Truth of who we are. Imagine that! Janet Conner did, and she encourages us to do the same, knowing all the while that these vows will continue to evolve in their meanings and purpose for our lives. Thank you, Janet Conner. Diving into *Soul Vows* has opened my heart even more than I thought was possible. My soul knows I AM forever free to be Me! Who wouldn't want everyone to feel that way?" —**Linda Linker Rosenthal,** transpersonal psychologist, author of *The Seven Chakra Sisters: Make Friends with the Inner Allies Who Keep You Healthy, Laughing, Loving, and Wise*

Other works by Janet Conner

Writing Down Your Soul

My Soul Page

The Lotus and The Lily

My Life Pages

Soul Vows

Gathering the Presence of the Divine in You,
Through You, and as You

JANET CONNER

Conari Press

This edition first published in 2015 by Conari Press, an imprint of Red Wheel/Weiser, LLC
With offices at:
665 Third Street, Suite 400
San Francisco, CA 94107
www.redwheelweiser.com

ISBN: 978-1-57324-642-2

Library of Congress Cataloging-in-Publication Data available upon request.

Cover design by Jim Warner
Cover photograph © Blackspring / Shutterstock
Interior by Jane Hagaman
Typeset in Mrs Eaves and Gill Sans Std
Chapter images by iStock | Sabonis
Author photograph © VonHenry Media, Inc
Graphics by Sandy Cromp, Sunshine Design Studio

Printed in the United States of America.
EBM
10 9 8 7 6 5 4 3 2 1

For you,

because your soul wants five things,
and one of them is to commit to values,

and your soul knows five things,
and one of them is there is a Presence inside you.

And for my Jerry,
whose soul vows set him free.

Each Soul Completes Me

My Beloved said, "My name is not complete
without yours."

And I thought: How could a human's worth
ever be such?

And God, knowing all our thoughts, and all
our thoughts are just innocent steps on the

path, then addressed my heart,

God revealed a sublime truth to the world
when He sang,

"I am made whole by your life. Each soul, each
soul completes Me."

—Hafiz, from *A Year with Hafiz,*
translation by Daniel Ladinsky

contents

Prelude

what your soul knows

There is a Presence inside you. There is a Presence inside everyone. Though you may have long ignored it, perhaps even willfully turned the other way, that divine Presence is alive and well and growing. It is a pulse, silently tapping out the rhythm of the ancient dance of longing for something more, something bigger, something to mark your every step as holy, important, and good. That Presence knows you. It knows who you are and who you long to be. It knows that the life of the Divine is your life, the love of the Divine is your love, and the Presence of the Divine is expressed in, and through, and as you. That Presence is now calling you to step into its tender embrace to learn the words and music and movements of your dance of divine Presence—Soul Vows.

welcome to your soul vows adventure

In 1997, my marriage disintegrated in rather dramatic fashion, and I was catapulted into a spiritual life I didn't know existed. At first, I did not recognize my divorce as a divine invitation; I was too angry and too frightened. I froze into a relentless state of panic. My one relief was a daily conversation with "Dear God" in my journal. Somehow, all that furious scribbling activated a wise, loving voice inside me. For three years, I turned to that voice every morning, sobbing out my story and begging for help. Help always came—sometimes through life, sometimes through dreams, sometimes through friends, but most consistently through the voice on the page. I began to trust that voice. I discovered there wasn't anything I could not say, any feeling I could not express, any fear I could not expose. I didn't know it at the time, but I was giving birth to the spiritual practice of deep soul writing.

One of the first topics I hashed out with "Dear God" was the sticky muck of vows. Marriage vows, I wrote, don't mean a damn thing! So are all vows suspect? Are vows by their very nature hopeless? Can a person ever declare vows that are true and holy and good? And live them—actually live them—always, forever?

A few days after I blasted out my questions, I stumbled upon *The House of Belonging*, one of David Whyte's early books of poetry. In the first few pages, I read a poem called "All the True Vows":

All the true vows
are secret vows
the ones we speak out loud
are the ones we break.

There is only one life
you can call your own
and a thousand others
you can call by any name you want.

Hold to the truth you make
every day with your own body,
don't turn your face away.

Hold to your own truth
at the center of the image
you were born with.

Those who do not understand
their destiny will never understand
the friends they have made
nor the work they have chosen

nor the one life that waits
beyond all the others.

By the lake in the wood
in the shadows
you can
whisper that truth
to the quiet reflection
you see in the water.

Whatever you hear from
the water, remember,

it wants you to carry
the sound of its truth on your lips.

Remember,
in this place
no one can hear you

and out of the silence
you can make a promise
it will kill you to break,

that way you'll find
what is real and what is not.

I know what I am saying.
Time almost forsook me
and I looked again.

Seeing my reflection
I broke a promise
and spoke
for the first time
after all these years

in my own voice,

before it was too late
to turn my face again.

The second I finished reading Whyte's "All the True Vows" I raced to my journal. "Dear God!" I wrote, "I know the vows I want! I want vows to *me*, to my *self*, to my *soul*, to *You!*" And with that declaration, my divine voice and I began long, intense conversations, diving deeper and deeper together into the well of my soul to find my true vows.

About a week into our conversation, I realized that before I could declare my new, true vows, I had to uncover and release the old underlying false vows—the fears and beliefs that had held me hostage since childhood. It took a lot of deep soul writing to excavate them, but once I'd dredged them up, looked them in the face, heard their stories, and thanked them for their service,

I was able to let them go. I prayerfully told each false vow, "You can go now," and—wonder of wonders—they left. For the first time in my life, I felt the genuine breath of freedom.

From this clean empty place, I was ready to call in my true vows. I sensed the import of what I was doing, so I didn't rush. I spent weeks in dialogue with "Dear God," talking over all the possibilities and trying some on for size.

At the same time, I was reading *Anatomy of the Spirit* by Carolyn Myss. Before reading it, I had viewed the chakras as an Eastern energy system that was intriguing, but also a tad confusing to my all-too-logical Western mind. After reading it, I couldn't miss the truth: the chakras are the beating heart at the center of humanity's diverse spiritual traditions. Weeks later, as I was reciting my final vows out loud one morning, I stopped halfway through and burst out laughing. I'd written seven vows that perfectly matched the seven chakras.

My new set of vows was the most exciting thing that had happened to me in years. I was on fire to share the joy of releasing my old, false vows and living my beautiful, new, true vows. It was time for a celebration. On November 11, 2000, ten women sat in a circle on my living room floor as I declared my vows publically for the first time. From then on, November 11 became a holy day. Each year on that date, I stop and reflect on how my soul vows have carried me through the past year and on all the deeper meanings they revealed.

November 11, 2010, was the tenth anniversary of my soul vows. To honor that special day, I drove to my favorite sacred place, St. Michael's Shrine in Tarpon Springs, Florida. There, I had a long written conversation with my divine voice. As I wrote, I realized I'd said my soul vows over three thousand times, and the more I said them and the more I lived them, the more gifts they bestowed and secrets they revealed.

"How can I thank you?" I wrote.

The answer was swift: "Teach it!"

And that's what I've done ever since.

Here are my soul vows. I speak them aloud every morning, adding the pronoun *I* in front of each. I pray my soul vows in the order of the chakras, from bottom to top.

Janet's Covenant

PRAY ALWAYS

SEEK TRUTH

SURRENDER, THERE IS NO PATH BUT GOD'S

COME FROM LOVE

HONOR MYSELF

LIVE IN PARTNERSHIP

UNITE TO CREATE GOOD

These words never fail to inspire or surprise me. On any given day, one of them will reveal a layer of meaning I never noticed before. Let me give you one example. For years when I said, "I come from love," I thought I was saying, "I, Janet, come from a state of love. I do my work with love. I write with love. I treat people with love. I emanate love." This was, forgive the pun, a lovely sentiment, but it also felt a bit like a burden. When I said this vow, I heard, "Gee, Janet, you *better* come from love, or you're not living your soul vows."

Then one morning, as I was staring at the words and speaking them aloud, I felt something shift in my heart. I stopped. My hands flew to my chest, and I burst into tears. "I come from love" doesn't mean I have to generate love; it means I was generated *by* Divine Love. Love doesn't come from *me*; it comes from my Divine Source. That's a huge difference in meaning—and it only took me nine years to realize it! This deeper understanding has led to a huge shift in how I live this vow.

Now, fourteen years into my relationship with my soul vows, I am beginning to see that the vows themselves were always breathing and living in a space of vast consciousness. They were always big. It is me who has slowly expanded my consciousness to meet them. I also see that they are a paradox. They came through my pen, but I didn't choose them. They chose me. They called to me from a future, expanded, potential self—my divine Self. And they beckon to me still, pointing the way to a deeper and deeper relationship with my self, my soul, my life, and my God. I long ago stopped pretending I know what my soul vows mean. I recognize them now as lifelong companions whose beauty and depth I can never exhaust.

From my story, you can see that soul vows bear little resemblance to business contracts, legal agreements, or even most marriage vows. Those kinds of human documents outline the promises, obligations, and responsibilities of the parties—who does what, what happens when they do, and what happens when they don't. Your soul vows are very different. They're simple. They're short. They don't require any details or definitions or clauses, and they don't lay out consequences. And yet these few simple phrases will carry you far beyond the benefits of any human partnership, all the way into the joys of divine partnership.

You might use the word *values* to describe your soul vows, but there's a vast difference between your soul's most precious values and the value statements you see posted on corporate walls. The latter are rarely referred to and, sadly, often have little influence on employee behavior. Soul vows, on the other hand, have meaning. Big meaning. Powerful meaning. Knock-your-socks-off meaning. You will refer to them every day of your life, and they will influence everything you do and every choice you make. They will become alive in you.

Your soul vows are also different from the popular values described in books such as Stephen Covey's *The Seven Habits of Highly Effective People* or Don Miguel Ruiz's *The Four Agreements*. These values are all smart and powerful and good, and following them creates a solid foundation for effective human interaction. But you are seeking a transmutation forged by an intimate and deeply personal relationship with the Divine, and these universal values, wise as they are, cannot carry you to the holy life that is yours and yours alone.

Your soul vows are not the same as your soul purpose. The two work seamlessly together and support one another, but they're not the same thing. Your soul purpose is your *why*—the destiny embedded in your being. Your soul vows are your *how*. They describe how you choose to walk this earth—not just at work or at home or in a relationship, but in every moment of every day. They are your grace points. They are how you receive and spread grace. As you live your soul vows, you become a fertile container in which the seed of your soul purpose can take root and flourish. If you long to know your soul's purpose, finding your soul vows is an ideal place to begin.

At first glance, soul vows appear to be a short list of qualities or behaviors. "Oh, great," you might think. "A *list*. How boring!"

But Mary Anne Radmacher, a creativity teacher and the most prolific artist and author I know, disagrees.

"A list is a door to seeing. A list is a door to knowing. A list is a door to deeper understanding," she says. But not just any list can be these things. In every creativity workshop she teaches, Mary Anne asks participants this question: "Which is a more successful shopping list—the one you make right before you walk out the door or the one you develop over days of noticing what you need?" The answer is always the same—the list you make over time. Why? Because as the awareness of need arises, you jot it down, which triggers you to remember it and then take action.

Noticing, memory, and urgency are all heighted by the simple act of making a list. Brain scientists recognize this honing of attention as a function of the reticular activating system (RAS). This is a good thing. Without our RAS, we'd be overwhelmed within minutes by a bombardment of stimuli, noise, and sensations. Thanks to our RAS, we can focus our attention to what matters, not to everyone, but to *us*. Hence the successful shopping list. In the coming chapters, as you develop your own soul vows, you'll come to appreciate the generative power of your own very focused soul vows list.

I titled my original soul vows list "Janet's Covenant." Soul vows are indeed a covenant—and an unshakable, unbreakable one at that. Do those words sound heavy? If you think in terms of human contracts, the word *covenant* can feel weighted with effort and obligation and consequences. But this is not a human covenant; it's a divine covenant—a sacred agreement between you and your divine Source. Soul vows aren't a list of obligations; they're a sweet love pact between your divine Self and your God. So of course they're unshakable. Why would anyone walk away from all that love? And they are unbreakable because they describe who you are at your core, your essence, your very soul. To break them, you would have to stop being you—and that, by definition, is impossible.

As lovely as a list and a divine covenant are, your soul vows are something even more. They are a *prayer*—a deeply personal, grace-inducing prayer. Over time, your soul vows will evolve into the most beautiful and powerful prayer of your day. When you speak your soul vows, four grace-filled things happen.

First, you renew your deep love for these ways of being. With each vow, you reenergize your commitment to live in alignment with your soul's most precious values. That alone lifts your spirit, triggers your RAS, focuses your attention, and influences your behavior. As you live your vows, you literally build who you are in this world, moving closer every day to your whole, authentic, holy Self.

Second, because your soul vows are a two-way covenant between you and your divine Source, as you declare them for yourself, you simultaneously activate divine response. As you speak a vow, you invite divine grace to move through you, creating a welcoming space for people and situations that are energetically aligned with that value, and—here's the most amazing part—simultaneously and effortlessly deflecting the people and situations that aren't. Over time you will find yourself surrounded by more and more of what is in sync with your vows and less and less of what isn't. This is how your soul vows change your world.

Third, your soul vows activate your inner mystic. I've asked dozens of spiritual leaders how they define mysticism, and they all agree it's a direct experience of the Divine. But please don't think that experience is reserved for the holy and the few. You were created a mystic. You are wired to directly experience your divine Source. That's why, no matter how many books or coaches or teachers talk about how to live an authentic life, a happy life, or one filled with meaning and purpose, there is still a persistent, lingering hunger. It's not a hunger for another program. It's not a hunger for a new advisor. It's not a hunger for a new way to control your thoughts, shift your emotions, or bring more balance into your life. It's not a hunger for another round on the self-improvement treadmill. It's not a hunger that can be satisfied reading a book or solving a problem in your mind. It's not a mental hunger. It's a hunger of the heart. It's a hunger of the soul.

It's a hunger for a tangible experience of the Divine.

Mystics of old understood this hunger. They marched off into seclusion to find it, face it, and feed it. They prepared themselves. They fasted. They chanted. They prayed. They meditated. They burrowed deep within their spirit and psyche to their very soul. And then it happened. They felt the divine embrace.

Most of us, today, don't want to run off to a monastery or ashram to satisfy that hunger. And we don't have to. We can plant our feet in our modern, wired, distracted, insanely busy lives *and* have a mystical experience of the living presence of the Divine. We can succeed at our jobs, pay our mortgages, raise our children, *and* live a holy life. Your soul vows are a very real and, in the end, quite simple way to walk into the mystical experience of the divine embrace. By the time you and your soul vows have become best friends, you will realize that you are a mystic.

Fourth, when you speak your soul vows, you are calling your full divine Self into this particular space-time experience. Your presence on this earth at this moment is *not* your total Self. It is an expression of that Self, one face of that Self, but it is not your full, multidimensional Self. Each time you speak a holy quality, you invoke more and more of your full Self to be present in your current human expression. Visualize your soul vows as stitches reaching through the space-time barrier to gather more and more of the wildly expansive Self that is your potential fullness. That fullness contains previous expressions of you, future expressions of you, and radiant facets of your share in divine Presence. Over time, as you live your soul vows, you weave together a larger, more fully present version of your Self on earth.

In the fourteenth century, Meister Eckhart described this transformation as "God must simply become me and I must become God—so completely that this 'he' and this 'I' share one 'is' and in this 'isness' do one work eternally" (*Breakthrough: Meister Eckhart's Creation Spirituality in New Translation* by Matthew Fox). A woman in a Soul Vows course described her "isness" transformation in slightly more modern terms: "Before soul vows, Wendy 1.0. After soul vows, Wendy 2.0!"

But your individual soul vows do something beyond building your *personal* expanded, 2.0 Self. As each of us calls our expanded divine Self into this space-time experience, together we build the *global* divine body. That's the real power of your soul vows and the real power that alters your experience here on earth. Soul vows are a living construction of a whole and holy Divine in you, through you, and as *you*, which builds collectively into the expression of the divine in *us*, through *us*, and as *us*.

Surely this is how we create heaven on earth.

Meet Your Soul Vows

the seven deep soul explorations

The seven deep soul explorations you will move through to discover, declare, and live your soul vows parallel the seven chakras. Because the energy and purpose of each exploration mirrors the energy and purpose of each chakra, the chakra system is a wonderful map to help you see where you are in the process, where you are going, and why you're going there.

Each of the seven chakra explorations will be explored in depth in the coming chapters, but let me give you an introductory taste, to inspire you to trust the natural progression of this sevenfold adventure and excite you to begin. Then, before you dive in, let me also give you some tips for how to get the most benefit from your journey.

Soul Vows and the Chakras

The concept of the chakra system is ancient, and, at first glance, these explorations may appear to be a new and rather modern application of the chakras' wisdom and grace. But with deeper reflection, I think you'll agree this is not new at all; indeed, this is a re-remembering of the mystical way we are constructed. Or as Hafiz, the great Sufi master, puts it:

Wayfarer,
Your body is my prayer carpet,

For I can see in your eyes

That you are exquisitely woven
With the finest silk and wool

And that Pattern upon your soul
Has the signature of God

And all your moods and colors of love
Come from His Divine vats of dye and Gold.

excerpt from "Exquisitely Woven," *I Heard God Laughing*,
translation by Daniel Ladinsky

If Hafiz were alive, he'd nod and laugh in recognition upon reading how Anoeda Judith describes the chakras in her classic book *Wheels of Life*:

The Tantric philosophies, from which the chakras emerge, are a philosophy of weaving. Their many threads weave a tapestry of reality that is both complex and elegant. Tantra is a philosophy that is both pro-life and pro-spiritual. It weaves spirit and matter back into its original whole, yet continues to move that whole along its spiral of evolution.

"Spirit and matter back into its original whole." That's it! That's what we want and where we're going. That's how we create heaven on earth. So how perfect that the chakras can carry us there.

The chakras are the universal and very beautiful story of the soul seeking union with the divine Beloved. In the ancient Vedic tradition, Shakti, who represents the divine feminine and the soul, longs for union with Shiva, who represents the divine masculine and the One. Shakti awakens with a feeling of longing and begins to travel through six experiences of duality, resolving each one as she goes, until at last she reaches the seventh plane, where she is reunited with her Beloved, Shiva. You will begin, as Shakti began, in the first chakra, and you will arrive, as Shakti arrived, united with the One in the seventh. The journey is a thrilling and holy deep soul adventure.

It is not an accident that the chakra system has seven distinct energy fields, and you will experience seven distinct deep soul explorations to reach sacred unity with the Divine in your soul vows. Seven has long been recognized as the number of totality and divinity. Consider the seven days of the week, seven seas, seven continents, seven colors in the rainbow, seven sacraments, seven days of creation, seven veils of Salome, seven candles on the Menorah, and many, many more. In *Numerology: The Power of Numbers*, Ruth Drayer tells us "the number seven represents spiritual completion." In *The Holy Trinity and the Law of Three*, Cynthia Bourgeault explains why seven is such a profound and necessary number: "[E]very developing process whatsoever must pass through seven distinct stages before it reaches its completion."

First Exploration
Honor Your Longing to Be One

In this initial exploration, you will awaken to your dual, royal lineage—fully human, fully divine. To create a container big enough and strong enough to support your journey through the chakras to become one with the One, you will begin to take loving care of yourself, feed yourself with high spiritual ideas, and become best friends with several vibrant spiritual practices. As you complete your exploration in this root chakra, you will know in every fiber of your being that you are ready for the big adventure ahead.

Second Exploration
Recognize the False Unconscious Vows That Have Kept You Fragmented

In this sacral-chakra exploration, you will uncover and acknowledge the falsehoods you've been telling yourself about yourself, and notice how those unconscious beliefs have kept you distracted and fragmented. You will sit with your false masters, learn their names, listen to their stories, and receive their surprising gifts. This all happens in the second chakra because all those roiling emotions in your gut have massive creative power. So far, you've been using that power unconsciously to create a life that isn't your authentic self and hasn't been a lot of fun. When you leave this chakra, you will be free.

Third Exploration
Gather Yourself into Wholeness

Your solar plexus chakra is the energy field of both your physical and spiritual centers of gravity. It holds your honor code, your personal power, and how you show up in the world. In the second chakra, you became aware of your false masters. Now, in the third, you will release them in a ceremony that you design yourself. As the ceremony ends, you will revel in the rare and exquisite feeling of being whole.

Fourth Exploration
Listen from Your Heart

When you release your false vows, you create room for your soul vows to make themselves known. This meeting takes place in the heart chakra because the heart is your primary organ of spiritual perception. Your spiritual heart—not your conscious mind—will identify the divine qualities that belong to you, introduce you to the Divine's role in your vows, and reveal how your soul vows gather the Presence of the Divine on earth. You'll know when your heart has chosen your vows because it will jump in ecstasy and tears of recognition will flow onto your cheeks. You will leave this chakra carrying your precious soul vows.

Fifth Exploration
Declare Your Soul Vows

In the throat chakra, you will explore the holy power of sound as your soul vows invite you to learn their sacred chant. Because the throat chakra holds the paradoxical energies of declaration and surrender, you will declare your soul vows with enthusiasm and joy, while at the same time surrendering to them, knowing you don't fully understand what they mean and or how they will direct your life. When you leave this chakra, you will have a new, thrilling personal spiritual practice born from your soul vows.

Sixth Exploration
Gather the Presence of the Divine

The sixth chakra is the energy field of the third eye, the center of knowing and light. As you live the soul vows that belong to you, you will gather more and more of the living Presence of the Divine in you, through you, and as you, bringing more divine light into the world. This is a mystery that never ends. Your third eye—your seat of inner knowing, attuned to divine truth—will support and guide you as the mysteries of life unfold. You and your soul vows will flow in this sixth-chakra energy for the rest of your life.

Seventh Exploration
Live in Sacred Unity

The seventh chakra is the seat of mystical communion with the Divine. As you live your soul vows day after day, year after year, you will no longer say your soul vows; you will *become* your soul vows. You will reach a state where you fully embody the facets of the Divine that are yours to express in the world. In this way, you become one with the One. Only the seventh chakra has the grace to support the mystery of divine union.

The seventh chakra is not the end of your soul's explorations. Instead, the most miraculous thing happens when you touch the holy energy of the seventh chakra. As you gather more and more and more of the divine Presence in you, through you, and as you in your daily life, you circle right back to the first chakra, your foundation, your grounding, your dual lineage. But this time you arrive with a whole new, joyous appreciation for who you truly are and who you came to be—the Presence of heaven on earth.

The chakra system is an exciting and helpful map, but in the end, your soul vows are a mystery. You think you choose them, but in truth, they choose you. You think you understand them, but years from now you will realize you are just beginning to discover how rich they are and what they really mean. So step into these explorations by setting aside any preconceived notions of what values you think you want to select or how your life will look when you are living them. If you try to identify your soul vows now, before you even begin, or if, as you proceed, you try to steer this ship the way *you* think it should go, you will miss the exquisite joy inherent in divine partnership, and you will not experience the beautiful changes you hoped for when you picked up this book.

How to Get the Most from Your Explorations

Soul vows are a mystical experience. They are a dance with the Divine. By definition, you can't control that or manage that or predict what will happen. And that's a good thing, because in the end, you don't want to. Because what you can control or manage or predict can only be as big or as beautiful as who you are right now and what you know right now. That's not good enough anymore. It won't take you anywhere new. And what you want at the soul level is to be more. More whole. More alive. More authentic. More holy. More of your divine Self.

So at the get-go, set aside your desire to control. If you have an overactive left brain—and we all do because modern society is wired to reinforce only left-brain logic, judgment, and measurement—tell your very logical, but for this adventure highly unnecessary, left brain to take a walk. Better still, tell it to take a vacation. How do you do that? Simple. You step down the volume of left-brain action activities and step up the volume of right-brain creation activities. That means:

Less media, more reading.

Less facts, more intuition.

Less consuming, more creating.

Less commotion, more solitude.

Less talking, more listening.

Less noise, more silence.

Less knowing, more unknowing.

Less doing, more being.

Less thinking ahead, more living in the now.

In other words, less controlling and more cooperating. Cooperating with whom? Why, with your soul and with your God. And here's the good news: this is not hard. Your soul already knows why you're here. It already knows why you're reading this book. It already knows how you long to commit to holy values. And it knows you are oh-so-ready to step onto the divine dance floor and let Spirit lead. Here are some specific ways you can let go of control and start cooperating with the Divine.

Have a Sense of Adventure

Acknowledge right now, before we begin, that you don't know what your soul vows will be, when you'll have them, or what exactly you'll do with them. You may not even know why you picked up this book. You may have simply felt a nudge and responded. So be brave. Show up. Be real. Follow where your soul leads. Let the adventure unfold.

Create Sacred Time and Space

Your soul vows are not a one-time writing prompt. If they were, you could sit down, ask for your soul vows on the page, and get up an hour later with your vows in hand. Honor the importance of your soul vows. Give them a sacred space in which they can come forward. Here are a few ways to do that:

Become friends with silence and solitude. There is no substitute for being alone with yourself. That is how and when you are open to divine guidance. But silence and solitude are the two things our consumer society does everything it can to get you to avoid. If you keep yourself busy talking, thinking, doing, going, buying, watching—all the ways we hold our souls at bay—you will miss messages bubbling up from your soul. So carve out time to be quiet. Once you fall in love with quiet, you will never go back to constant bustle.

Engage in daily prayer. Your soul vows will become the most important prayer of your life. So this is a good time to strengthen your relationship with prayer. Return to the prayers of your spiritual or cultural tradition, if you like. Or embrace the prayer practices of other traditions. Or create a new prayer practice of your own. Find one that makes your heart sing. However you do it, become best friends with prayer.

Set aside time for deep soul writing. The questions you will explore in *Soul Vows* go deep, probably deeper than you've ever gone. Give yourself significant blocks of time for writing, reflection, and creating a space in which your soul can be heard.

Set aside time to read. You will select a master-teacher companion book to walk with you throughout this process. Many of your most startling insights will come as you absorb the words of your special teacher. Set aside time to read every day.

Give attention to what is sacred to you. You may look at your life and think you're too busy to set aside time for writing and reading. But you're not too busy; you're too distracted. Do you know the difference? Here's the simple but painful truth: what you give your attention to is what you deem sacred. Say that out loud: "What I give my attention to is sacred to me." So what are you giving your attention to? Identify ten or twelve activities that get the bulk of your time. Then ask yourself for each, "Is this sacred? Is this holy? If not, why have I carved out so much of my precious time for it?" Then try it in the reverse. Ask yourself, "What's truly important to me?" and write that list. Then count how many hours or minutes those people or activities get. Put those two lists side by side. There in front of you is a clear graphic of the life you have created versus the life you wish you were living. This simple self-evaluation exercise will help you rearrange your life in ways that will have momentous and lasting effects.

Be Willing to Enter the Mystery

The soul can't be explained or understood. It is, after all, your divine Self, and divinity is wild, untamable, and more vast and magnificent than our minds can grasp. Whatever idea or image you hold in your mind of the soul or the Divine is by definition too small. That's perhaps why we feel so compelled to explore these fields of the soul. We long for the mystery. So acknowledge that you are stepping into a mystery, and although that may feel strange, even a bit dangerous, know that all is well because you are guided and held at the deepest level.

Trust Yourself and Trust the Process

A month from now, a year from now, a decade from now, you will look back and feel boundless gratitude for yourself for setting aside the space and time to receive your soul vows. But the only way you can get to that future day of joy is to walk the path now, explore the fields now, enter the mystery now. Even if you're not sure what that means or what will happen, start walking. Trust that your spiritual feet know exactly what they're doing and where they're going. The path is actually brightly lit, if we see with the eyes of our souls.

Make Friends with Paradox

In each of the seven chakra explorations, you will stumble upon a head-scratching paradox.

At first, paradox can seem wildly frustrating because it poses an unanswerable question: how can two diametric opposites both be true at the same time? For example, consider my favorite paradox from Meister Eckhart: "to be full, you must be empty." Got that? If I'm empty, how am I full? And if I'm full, how can I be empty? It feels like trying to maneuver one boat named *Full* and another named *Empty* into the same slip. Impossible, right? But in the mystical realm paradox is not only not impossible, it's a truth at the center of life.

The secret to "solving" a paradox is to shift your view of the friction between two apparent opposites from a search for a solution to an invitation into divine mystery. While two boats can't enter the same space, two wafts of perfumes can and two colored lights can. With scent and light, the two opposites effortlessly merge and create something new, something exciting, a third thing unique unto itself. A triangle is the perfect shape to demonstrate this mystery of paradox. If one side of the triangle is one statement and the opposite side is the opposite statement, then the base of the triangle is not the winner of the two; it's something new altogether.

In *The Holy Trinity and the Law of Three*, Cynthia Bourgeault explains what happens as we wrestle with paradox:

> In contrast to a binary system, which finds stability in the balance of opposites, the ternary system stipulates a third force that emerges as the necessary mediation of these opposites and that in turn (and this is the really crucial point) generates a synthesis at a whole new level. It is a dialectic whose resolution simultaneously creates a new realm of possibility.

Dialectic, by the way, means "a discourse between opposites; a way of resolving disagreements not by debating to prove a point or to win, but by exploring metaphysical contradictions to find new solutions." As you wrestle with the two sides of the triangle of paradox in each of the chakras, you will discover a previously unknown third side and a whole new realm of possibility.

To help you capture these revelations, each exploration will end with a discussion of the major paradox of that chakra and a blank triangle on which you can record your dialectic conversation with yourself and the beautiful new idea that arose as a result.

Put Your Discoveries in Your Pocket

You will make seven major discoveries in your soul vows adventure, one at the end of each chakra exploration. These are treasures that will carry you for the rest of your life. To help you remember them and hold them in your heart, set aside a "Discovery" page or two at the front of your journal and add each discovery to what will become a very holy list. As you make each of the seven discoveries, add them in some way to your prayer practices.

Get into Theta

Many of your experiences in *Soul Vows* will come through deep soul writing. If you are journaling—not soul writing—you could miss access to the depth of wisdom waiting for you a hair below conscious mind. To touch that wisdom, you want to access the theta brain-wave state. Here are the seven steps for getting into theta through soul writing:

1. Set your intention to connect with your divine voice. You do this by simply having the desire to go beneath and beyond your conscious mind, connect with yourself at the soul level, and activate your own extraordinary voice of wisdom and grace. Don't skip over this split-second step. It sets the whole miraculous chain in motion.

2. Address the voice by name. If you have an ongoing soul writing practice, you have a personal term of

endearment for your divine partner. If you are new to soul writing or don't yet have a name, begin to experiment with "Dear One," "Dear Beloved," "Dear Friend," or simply write, "Dear Voice." Eventually your personal and private name will make itself known.

3. Write by hand. It is possible to get into theta on the computer, but looking at a screen pulls most of us back into conscious mind. Write with a pen so you feel the presence of your internal voice in your hand. If you cannot hold a pen, look into voice-recognition software.

4. Activate all five senses:

   - Vision is automatically engaged as you look at the page.

   - The parts of your brain responsible for hearing are firing even if you write in total silence, but if you want to add sound, play sacred music, ancient mantras, meditative chants, or the *Theta Music* CD (available at janetconner.com).

   - Touch is obviously engaged.

   - Activate the sense of smell, your most powerful sense, with essential oils, flowers, candles—anything that appeals to you.

   - Drink pure water after you write. With each sip, speak aloud a blessing or guidance that came through your soul writing. Drinking the grace-infused water brings the wisdom and insights into your body at the cellular level.

5. Ask lots of open-ended questions. In *Writing Down Your Soul* there is extensive information on questions that activate the voice and questions that don't.

6. Write fast, without editing or judging. This is how you leave your critical conscious mind sputtering in the distance. If you're feeling stuck, pick up the speed of your writing.

7. Be grateful. Say thank you.

You will need a journal for this adventure, so this is the ideal time to get *My Soul Pages* or *My Life Pages*, two journals designed for deep soul writers. The seven steps for getting into theta are explained in more detail in both journals.

Pace Yourself

Go through the seven explorations at the pace that feels right to you. When I teach Soul Vows, my live global telecourse, each exploration lasts one week, but there is no set amount of time. Tune into your own soul to know when you're ready to dive deeper and when you're ready to move on. Most people will have the wording of their personal soul vows in five to six weeks. After that, it will take a lifetime to discover what they really mean.

Keep Your Commitment

Soul vows are not a toe dip in the spiritual waters. The seven explorations are not a self-help exercise promising that if you do X, you'll get Y. Discovering your soul vows is making a mystical dive into deep waters that aren't always clear and swimming toward a destination that isn't always visible. That might sound a bit scary, but the hidden mystery is actually what makes this path so personal, so exquisite, and so beautiful. This is an opportunity to explore at the deepest levels who you can be in this earth experience. So if the going should get a little rough, know that it's OK, and stay the course. Beauty, divine beauty, awaits. Carry this sweet truth with you as you begin:

I searched for God and found only myself.
I searched for myself and found only God.

Sufi proverb

honor your longing to be one

First Chakra: Root Chakra
First Paradox: I am human; I am divine.
First Discovery: I am ready.

*Once the soul awakens, the search begins . . .
you are inflamed with a special longing
that will never again let you linger in the lowlands
of complacency and partial fulfillment.
The eternal makes you urgent.*

John O'Donohue, *Anam Cara*

What do you long for? Have you asked yourself this question? We constantly ask ourselves what we want. But *want* is too small a verb for this soul vows exploration, because in our consumption-obsessed world, *want* is invariably paired with a *thing*. When your parents asked your four-year-old self what you wanted for your birthday, you knew they were asking for a thing like a toy or a book or a bike. Later, *want* became paired with larger and more expensive things, like a car, a house, a raise. This material solution to wanting is so ingrained that even our spiritual practices have been subverted by supposedly secret formulae that somehow manipulate the universe to give us what we want.

The verb *want* actually stretches across a vast range of meanings, from the smallest ("I want a sandwich") to substantive needs ("I want a better job)" to soul-directed desires ("I want to spend more time painting") all the way to heart yearnings ("I want to see my mother before she dies"). But then, somewhere beyond yearning, *want* leaps a fence into *longing*. This is territory we rarely visit. Our consumer culture doesn't have a clue what to do with longing, because longing can't be satisfied with more stuff. The truth is, if we acknowledge what we really want—*what we long for*—our priorities will shift, and all the things in the material world will never satisfy us again.

I know. I jumped that fence on December 31, 1995. I was in a toxic marriage and doing lucrative but soul-vacant work. I was sitting in my back-bedroom office, feeling fragmented, disconnected, and parched, and I thought, "I cannot bear another year like this." In some place deep in my heart, I knew that even if I reinvigorated my marriage and succeeded wildly at my career, I would still be hungry, because what I really wanted was more God.

I grabbed a piece of paper and scribbled, "I want You to find me. I will sit in a field until You find me." I could see myself sitting on the ground in a barren field, surrounded by nothing but dry golden grass for miles, nothing but hot yellow sky above. God could not miss me, if God would only look!

I stared at the paper, sighed, and tucked it in my desk drawer. I stood up, resigned to living another year just like the one before.

But that's not what happened. My cry of longing set something in motion. Within months, my marriage, my house, my clients, my savings—everything I'd labored so hard to collect— began tumbling out of my grip. The losses were brutal, but out of the ashes of my old life, small green shoots of a much more satisfying life began to appear. In the darkest days of the divorce, I discovered deep soul writing. That led me to write the book *Writing Down Your Soul*. Facing bankruptcy, I stumbled upon the original teachings of Buddha and Jesus on how to nourish a truly beautiful and abundant life. That led me to write *The Lotus and The Lily*. Then, on an ordinary January morning in 2011, I was awakened with the startling news "Your soul wants five things" in my left ear. I thought that Spirit might want to pick a more successful author for this assignment, but by the end of the day, I was in my office, laying out the five courses and five books in a series called *Your Soul Wants Five Things*.

Then, as I was beginning to write this book, I was invited to lead a weekend of events for five Unity churches in Iowa. The region kindly put me up at PrairieWoods, a Franciscan retreat center in Cedar Rapids. I decided to give myself a day of silence, to gather my strength for the two full days of speaking and teaching to come. I walked the lovely paths through the woods and found myself in front of an eleven-circuit labyrinth set in a large field surrounded by trees.

As I entered the labyrinth, I took a deep breath and released all my concerns about the weekend. With each step, I whispered over and over again, "I let go, I let go, I let go." When I reached the center, I sat down on a little wooden stool someone had placed over a large stone. I had no thoughts, no desires, not even any prayers. I just sat there, feeling the fall sun on my face and watching the dance of the wind releasing bursts of golden leaves. After ten minutes or so, I heard as clearly, as if someone were standing in front of me, "Your soul wants one thing." I smiled at the empty space before me. Of course. We all want the same thing—the one thing. We all want more God. We all long to be one with the One.

On the flight back home, I stared out the plane window, watching Iowa recede, and saw myself again on that stool in the middle of a field. Suddenly I realized I could release the prayer I'd been holding in my heart for eighteen years: "You found me! You found me! I sat in a field, and You found me!"

All spiritual paths lead to Oneness. Of that I'm certain. The awakened one in Buddhism, the incarnated one in Christianity, the chosen one in Judaism, the unified divine feminine and masculine in Hinduism, the enfolding love of the hidden treasure in Islam. I love to read the sacred texts and mystical poetry of all traditions, but sometimes, when I'm hungry for a few elegant sentences to carry me into a living experience of the divine embrace, I reach for the sonorous voice of the Celts, John O'Donohue, and the soothing voice of the Sufis, Kabir Helminski. They always open my heart a little wider. And they always let a little more of that Oneness in.

Listen to this quote from *Living Presence* by Helminski: "Spiritual attainment is a fundamental transformation of the 'I' from a separate, limited, and contracted identity into a rich and infinite one. It is a movement from separation to union."

"Separation to union"—that's it in just three words.

Now listen to what John O'Donohue says in *Beauty*: "Spirituality has to do with the transfiguration of distance, to come near to ourselves, to beauty and to God. At the heart of spirituality is the awakening of real presence."

To come near. So near we can touch beauty, touch God, and awaken to real presence. To be one. To be whole. *That's* why you're here. That's why I'm here. And that's the heart of soul vows.

So my question for you, as you step into this profound adventure, is, *what do you long for?* Not, what do you want? When you look beyond wanting and even beyond yearning, when you leap over that invisible fence, where do you land? What is your heart's deepest desire? Put it on paper like I did. You will undoubtedly use different words, but I'm willing to bet that your heart is hungry for the same thing I was hungry for—the same thing we're all hungry for—to be found, to be touched, to be whole, to be one with the One.

It may seem counterintuitive, but we begin our explorations of this divine union in the first chakra at the base of the spine. We tend to look at the chakra system and think the point of the spiritual life is to reach the "higher" chakras, especially the inner knowing of the sixth and the divine consciousness of the seventh. But the way to the seventh chakra begins right here in this very grounded, very human, and often messy first chakra.

This is where you absorbed your initial sense of belonging in the world and your first identity. Your immediate family was your first "we." That small "we" quickly expanded to include your neighborhood, culture, spiritual tradition, class, race, and ethnic heritage. That big "we" formed the words you said, the thoughts you held, the foods you ate, and the ideas you believed. Surrounded and immersed in the norms and expectations and values and fears of your surroundings, you swallowed, you got in line, you conformed, you obeyed. Your singular self, your small "I," was subsumed into a communal and very powerful "we."

With all that complex history, probably going back generations, it is not surprising that this root chakra hosts a few issues. In the second chakra, you will have many opportunities to hear and heal the stories and patterns of your life, but for now, simply recognize that your soul is longing for a deeper, fuller membership in its before-this-family family—the divine "We." Remember, the first chakra is where Shakti's story begins. The ancient story says that Shakti and Shiva were once so completely fused together that they had no experience of one another. They separated in order to see one another and know one another and experience the delicious feeling of longing for one another. The chakra story is the story of Shakti's journey back to her Beloved. This first chakra is where your story begins, too.

And now, you are ready. You are ready to step forward. You are ready to dive in. You are ready, just like Shakti, to again be one with the One.

Deep Soul Explorations

In this first deep soul exploration in the first chakra, you will:

- take sweet care of yourself
- infuse your spirit with high spiritual ideas
- set up vibrant spiritual practices

Take Sweet Care of Yourself

To a Celt or Native American or member of any earth-based tradition, the idea of the duality of body and soul would be comical. To our early ancestors, a person was not a body with a soul; a human was an integrated body-soul. But over time, as duality-laden religions dominated the culture, we lost touch with this inner knowing. We stopped seeing the body as the beautiful expression of spirit. John O'Donohue speaks of this truth in his book *Anam Cara: A Book of Celtic Wisdom*: "The body is your only home in the universe. It is your house of belonging here in the world. It is a very sacred temple. To spend time in silence before the mystery of your body brings you toward wisdom and holiness."

The first chakra—the chakra that energetically grounds your sacred temple to mother earth—is the ideal place to begin these seven deep soul explorations, because your soul vows are the vehicle through which you will gather divine Presence in you and through you. That means in and through your body. You won't just *think* your soul vows or *say* your soul vows; you will *be* your soul vows. You will be your soul vows in the most ordinary times and ordinary ways. Through your hands and your feet, you will plant your vows on earth. So take time in this first exploration to refresh your relationship with this exquisite vehicle of earthly life, your body.

Begin with Self-Care

The word *self-care* has been bandied about so much that we don't really hear it anymore. Caring for ourselves comes across as one more thing to do, one more retreat to attend, one more yoga series to sign up for. That's a great shame because self-care—caring for your Self—is the first way we acknowledge that we are the beloved of the Divine. If we are as loved as the poet-saints tell us, then we honor the embrace of the Divine by embracing ourselves.

The popular wording for this whole-self embrace is "body, mind, spirit." But there's an intrinsic problem with that phrase. It reinforces a feeling of parts—the body part, the mind part, the spirit part. We are not a series of parts; we are an integrated whole. Honoring the body is one and the same as honoring the mind, and one and the same as honoring the spirit.

An exciting way to begin to honor your exquisite body is to turn your attention to your senses, because, as John O'Donohue reminds us in *Anam Cara,* "Your senses link you intimately with the divine within you and around you." As you focus on, appreciate, and begin to honor your miraculous senses, something surprising and holy happens: you begin to notice that divine guidance flows effortlessly and continuously in and through them. Throughout your entire body, but especially in your gut, you awaken to your natural gift of clairsentience and realize you are, and always have been, a font of intuition. That's what "I have a gut feeling" means.

With practice, you can learn to trust the yes and no signals in your body. As you revel in your sense of vision, for example, you will begin to notice divine guidance everywhere you look. Animals crossing your path, books opening to a particular page, even billboards will surprise you with news that you are guided and loved. When you reduce the amount of noise bombarding your ears, you will begin to hear guidance all around. It may come as a snippet of conversation, a phrase in a song, the call of an owl. You don't know what it will be or how it will come, but by becoming quiet and open, you will begin to hear in a whole new way. These are just a few of the gifts that come from wrapping yourself in your own self-loving embrace.

Here are some ways you can take sweet care of yourself during this first deep soul exploration. Each ends with a few deep soul writing questions that may help you activate your own internal wisdom.

Notice the Media You Invite into Your Life

Your attention is sacred. Where it lands is what you deem holy. Notice the images, ideas, and emotions that pour into you through the media you watch, the music you listen to, and the newspapers, magazines, and books you read. Once you pay attention, you may find that some, perhaps most, are not in alignment with what your soul knows to be true.

Don't worry if this happens. Don't get mad at yourself. Simply stop and listen to your internal knowing and act on the truth you hear.

Where does my attention land throughout my day?

What is that telling me about what I consider holy?

Reduce the Noise in Your Life

You can tune into your internal knowing more easily with a body that is not bombarded with noise. Every sound, from the softest sigh to the roar of a jet engine, is a vibration, and your body feels them all, whether you are conscious of it or not. Noise is not just a nuisance; it's a health hazard impacting hearing loss, hypertension, heart disease, aggression, and sleep. But it's tough to get away from. Our consumer-oriented world intentionally uses noise to induce us to buy things. The next time you walk into a store, notice the rhythm and volume of the songs on the sound system. Stores don't play this music to entertain, and it's not background music. It's in your face—or rather, in your ear—because research shows that people spend more money when high energy music is playing at high volume.

Restaurants are often worse. We go out to eat for respite, food, and conversation, but instead of creating an environment conducive to enjoyment, many restaurants, especially large chains, serve up surround-sound assault. The music prevents conversation and often insults the cuisine. When my favorite Thai restaurant played loud country music, I walked out, never to return. Find the quiet mom-and-pop restaurants in your area and encourage your friends to support them, too. And tell your dentist and doctor and car repair shop to please turn the TV down or, better still, off.

You may not be able to get away from all the exterior noise in your life, but you can control interior noise. Often, instead of creating quiet havens in our private spaces, we add to the noise by playing the radio in the car, keeping ear buds in our ears, and leaving the TV on. In honor of your precious body and delicate sense of hearing, notice the noise in your life and eliminate all you can. Then watch as your muscles untense in the quiet, and guidance begins to flow more easily in and through your beautiful, relaxed body.

How much noise is there in my life?

How does noise affect me? Have I become immune to noise?

Am I afraid of what might happen in the quiet?

How can I create more quiet?

Observe How You Spend Time

People constantly tell me they want to read more books, spend more time with sacred texts, and take more soul-lifting courses. They want more prayer and meditation. They want to get outside more, move their body more, and so many other wonderful things. But after they list all the lovely things they want, they invariably say, "But I can't. There isn't enough time. I'm too busy." Then they ask me what they can do to have a more soulful life.

I smile, knowing how this conversation will end, but I gamely tell the truth: "The single thing that has had the most dramatic and beautiful impact on my life is giving up TV." This is not the answer they're expecting, and it's certainly not the answer they want. With shock and often sadness in their eyes they say, "I can't do that."

I didn't think I could either. I can't even take credit for giving up TV; it wasn't my idea. I was in Oaxaca, Mexico, four years ago, leading a soul-writing retreat, when I realized that my mind had finally stopped wandering away, and I was focused only on the people I was with, the food I was relishing, and the experiences we were having. I rushed to my hotel room, grabbed a pen, and begged on the page, "Help me remember this! Help me live like this when I get home!" Five days later, back in Florida, I turned on the TV, and the screen was black. Just in case I missed the point, the cable line was dead, too. At first, I was annoyed.

A few days later, I realized, "Wait a minute! This is what I asked for!" I called the cable company to take the box. I thought I'd miss the few shows I liked. But the oddest thing happened. Not only did I not miss anything, but I also discovered astonishing amounts of new time in the evening. This "found time" makes it possible for me to read my guests' books for *The Soul-Directed Life*, the online radio show that I host; listen to lengthy talks by teachers I admire; and do massive amounts of research for my courses and books.

I found time by eliminating TV, but that's not the only way. You might find time by cutting back on meetings or volunteering, not going out for lunch, turning down invitations, staying home on weekends, paying someone to clean the house. In other words, if you don't really want to do something, say no.

How will you know where to find time? Ask your gut; your body knows. Time is a holy gift. Love yourself enough to give yourself more of it.

Do I treat time like a holy gift? Where do I spend my twenty-four hours?

Is there a disconnect between what I say is important and what I do?

Do I watch too much TV? Do I spend too much time online?

Where can I find time?

Deep in my gut, what do I want to say no to?

Get More Sleep

One of the first things to do with your newfound time is sleep. Forty million people in the United States have chronic sleep disorders. This is a serious problem. While you're sleeping, your body heals and your brain reorganizes circuits to build long- and short-term memory. Per the National Sleep Foundation, "Sleep affects how we look, feel and perform on a daily basis, and can have a major impact on our overall quality of life." Most adults need seven to nine hours, yet only 29 percent of adults get even six. And those six might be more anxious than restful. Sleep deprivation is used as torture, so why do we do it to ourselves and then brag about how we get by on so little sleep? Be kind to yourself. Get more sleep.

Do I remember what it feels like to be well rested?

How much sleep do I give myself?

Do I treat self-inflicted sleep deprivation as a badge of honor?

What needs to change so I can give myself more sleep?

Pay Attention to How Your Body Responds

Your body is an energetic tuning fork and a very reliable one. When something happens, notice where you feel a reaction in your body and honor that feedback. Don't let anyone push you to do something you don't want to do, watch something you don't want to watch, or go somewhere you don't want to go. The days of obeying other people's desires over your own sacred intuition are over. Do only what feels aligned with the truth of your soul.

What did I do today, yesterday, last week, last month that I didn't want to do?

How did I know I didn't want to do it? Did my body tell me no?

Where does my body register the guidance of no?

Move Your Body

Are you starting to fall in love with your divinely designed body? I hope so. To help you appreciate what a magnificent gift your body is, move more. Go to a yoga, tai chi, or other movement class. Take a walk, go for a swim, get a massage, get up and stretch, dance around the kitchen, or simply raise your arms in gratitude to the sun. Do *something* to experience the joy of a body that moves.

Do I love my body? And do I love it just the way it is?

How do I feel when I move? Do I want more movement?

What needs to change so I can move more?

Nourish Your Body

Notice what you put into your beautiful body. Begin by increasing the amount of pure water you drink. Water is the elixir of life. It nourishes every cell and flushes out toxins and waste. You can make room for more water by eliminating sugared and diet drinks. If you need help doing this, simply promise yourself you'll read the label out loud before you take the first sip. If you see the words *high fructose corn syrup* or *aspartame* (or any other chemical sugar substitute), your body will tell you to put it down. Don't take my word for it; listen to your beautiful clairsentient body.

And give your holy body holy food. There are thousands of books by diet gurus who are only too happy to tell you what you should eat. If you want to read any of them, go right ahead. But here's a simple, one-second, cost-nothing way to know. When you reach for something to eat, imagine the Divine feeding it to you like you would feed your precious baby. That makes things pretty clear, doesn't it?

Would the Beloved feed me what I feed myself?

What needs to change so that I give myself more holy water and food?

Relish Your Food

Food is a sacrament. Marc David, founder of the Institute for the Psychology of Eating, the world's leading school in nutritional psychology, wrote, "Eating is life. Each time we eat, the soul continues its earthly journey. With each morsel of food swallowed a voice says, 'I choose life. I choose to eat, for I yearn for something more.'" You can see this phenomenon play out clearly in people who are close to death. They let you know they're no longer interested in living by turning their head and refusing to eat.

Do you choose life today? If so, open your mouth and savor the sacrament of eating.

Do I choose life?

Is food a sacrament?

Bless Your Food

No matter what you're eating, bless it—yes, even a drive-through hamburger. Before I eat anything, I rub my hands together briskly and hold them over the food, palms down, with my two hands forming an open triangle. I move the triangle in a circle over the plate, and looking through the triangle say out loud, "Thank you, Mother, for the gifts I have been given. May this food enter my body for my health, well-being, protection, and joy." You are welcome to this blessing, but why not write your own?

Before dinner, I also randomly open the book *A Grateful Heart.* Somehow the mealtime blessing my eye lands on is always exactly what I need to remember. And when friends come for dinner, we pass the book around. On special occasions, we write our name and the date beside the blessing we read aloud. Later, when I open *A Grateful Heart* again, sweet memories pop off every page.

How shall I bless my food?

Go Outside

Your soul made the choice to be here on this beautiful blue planet. Honor that choice by spending more time in nature. Begin by simply stepping outside. Sit in the sun for a bit. Go for a long, slow walk. Feel the breeze. Hear the birds. Smell the air. For now, earth is your home. Love and appreciate it.

How do I feel when I go outside?

How can I spend more time in nature?

Honor Your Sanctuary

The law of subtraction is always talking to us, but we don't always listen. Look at your bedroom, kitchen, bathroom, office, car. If there is clutter and confusion, use a bit of your newfound time to clear and clean. The quality of your space does influence what happens in that space.

Do I love my bedroom, my work space, my kitchen—wherever I spend time?
How can I treat my space as sacred space?

Protect Your Soul Light

We think of Spirit as energy and light, but we forget sometimes that we too are energy and light. The mass culture is energy, too, but it vibrates at a different frequency.

I had a visceral reminder of this when I was invited to teach soul writing for a small group on a cruise ship. As the ship pulled away from the dock, the PA system ordered all two thousand passengers to go to their assigned muster stations for a safety briefing. I set off to find my station, feeling lighthearted and happy. As I worked my way through the progressively more crowded hallways, I felt jostled first from the left and then from the right. I looked around. Scads of people were rushing past me, but no one was touching me. Standing in line for dinner that night, I looked around to see who was bumping into me. No one was. That night I fell into my bunk, utterly exhausted.

By the time I got home four days later, I was sick. Even with twelve hours of sleep every night plus afternoon naps, I wasn't getting better. This made no sense, so I called Margo Mastromarchi, a gifted angel guidance reader, for a little guidance. What I got from the angels was a lecture on vibration and a stern reminder to protect my soul light. Now, even if I'm just going to my friendly neighborhood post office, as I'm turning the key in my door, I call upon Archangel Michael to surround me with a protective layer of sapphire blue light. As I start the car, I ask for protection for me and for everyone on the road. As I drive, I send a blessing to the people I'll meet and the places I'll visit.

Go within and find your own method to protect your precious soul light; then let it become an automatic habit of self-love.

What people or places drain my energy? How do I perceive that?
What is my personal blessing of protection?

Infuse Your Spirit with High Spiritual Ideas

I am not your teacher. I say this to shift attention away from me and onto the teachers who know you best—your life, your soul, your big divine Self, and your loving inner voice. In addition, I recommend you spend time with the words of masters and mystics across time. They know the way to the One. You can do that in a simple, inexpensive way by choosing a book or sacred text and reading just a bit from it every day. And I do mean just a bit. A few lines, a paragraph, one verse—that's really all you need to, or want to, absorb in one sitting. In the presence of a great soul, you will find you simply can't turn the page; you are compelled to stop and slowly digest the words.

There's a beautiful book on how to read this way, *Lectio Divina* by Christine Valters Paintner. Paintner is a Benedictine Oblate who follows the practice of *lectio divina*—divine reading—as described by St. Benedict, the sixth-century founder of Western monasticism. The practice has four consecutive actions: first, read the words for understanding; second, listen for deeper meaning; third, repeat the words aloud to savor the text; and finally, rest in the stillness. The practice of reading this way has ancient roots in the Jewish practice of *haggadah*, repeating a passage softly until it is learned by heart. The Qur'an, which has been passed down orally for centuries, has been memorized this way. And in the Hindu and Buddhist traditions, a mantra or sacred utterance is repeated aloud, over and over, releasing layers of mystical illumination with each repetition. If you'd like to know more about this approach to divine reading, I highly recommend *Lectio Divina*.

It is also possible that your soul already knows how to read this way. Mine does. Here's how I read mystical poetry or a sacred text or the work of a master teacher:

1. Read slowly. Don't rush. One page may be more than enough.

2. When you come across a sentence or phrase or word that knocks on your heart, stop and reread it. If it feels important, underline or highlight or somehow mark the page so you can find it again.

3. Look up from the book and speak the words aloud several times as you stare off in space. Don't try to figure out any meaning; just listen to the words.

4. Just sit in the silence, staring off into space. After your attention naturally returns to normal, you might go back to the page and make sure you underlined the phrase. (I also write the page number and a word or two about what I read on the inside of the book's front cover. That way, when I want to find a particular idea or sentence again, I can simply glance at the inside cover.)

Is this lectio divina? It may not quite abide by St. Benedict's instructions, but I think it fits his purpose—to "listen with the ear of our heart."

In just two lines, Rumi tells us how to read this way and why doing so is so important. Why don't you begin your *lectio divina* practice repeating these words a few times:

> Being in a hurry throws the key on the ground
> to a door I want you to enter.
>
> If you read my words slowly and out loud, they
> will help to pick the lock.

"Pick the Lock" from *Purity of Desire*, translation by Daniel Ladinsky

To learn how your soul listens with the ear of your heart, simply notice how you naturally react when you read something beautiful or holy. Do you stop reading? Do you suck in your breath? Do you find yourself mouthing the words or whispering them out loud? Do you touch your face, your heart, your mouth? Do you

soul vows

stare off in space? Close the book? Close your eyes? Listen to your body. It knows how to partake of a feast of holy words.

That feast can include holy images as well. Several members of my Soul Vows courses have engaged in *visio divina*—divine looking—by spending time with holy images, icons, mandalas, and books filled with soul-stirring art.

How do you select the master-teacher companion to walk with you on this soul vows journey? Go inside and see if you feel called to spend time with a sacred text such as the Torah, the Holy Bible, the Bhagavad Gita, the Upanishads, the Qur'an, or the Pali Canon.

Or perhaps you feel a longing to get to know a mystic of old. I wish I could go back to the fourteenth century, sit in a pew in Germany, and hear Meister Eckhart's radical sermons on the union of the soul and God. In a way I can, thanks to Matthew Fox's brilliant commentaries in *Breakthrough: Meister Eckhart's Creation Spirituality in New Translation*. Or perhaps you feel called to spend time with a modern mystic such as Thomas Merton, Joel Goldsmith, Cynthia Bourgeault, or Meher Baba. Or perhaps you'd like to absorb the book Dr. Martin Luther King Jr. took with him to prison, *Meditations of the Heart* by Howard Thurman. Perhaps a mystical poet such as Hafiz or Rumi is calling you to sit down and become best friends.

Look at your bookshelves. Three years ago, I stood in front of the bookshelf that holds my most beloved spiritual treasures, looking for the perfect companion for the Soul Vows course. I thought I knew all the books in this bookcase intimately, but as my eye ran over the spines, I suddenly noticed a faded gold paperback, *Anam Cara*. I didn't know what the book was about or who John O'Donohue was, and I had no memory of buying it. How long had *Anam Cara* been sitting on my own shelf, waiting for me? I don't know. I can only say thank you to the sweet nudge from my soul that compelled me to buy it years before I was ready to read it. See if there is a book like that waiting on your shelf for you.

Or you might feel called to reread an old friend—a friend you sense has more to teach you on second or third reading. Or you might feel the urge to wander around a bookstore and see what grabs your attention. Whatever your method, seek something deep—something that will carry you into new territory, something or someone who will speak to you at the deepest soul level. Select something rich—a truffle, not a candy bar—that you can savor slowly.

Here are a few books that have expanded the hearts and minds of members of previous Soul Vows courses. But don't choose a book because I or someone else recommends it. Ask your own soul for guidance and it will be provided.

Prose (some are also available as recordings)

Living Presence or *The Knowing Heart,* Kabir Helminski

Autobiography of a Yogi or *Divine Romance,* Paramahansa Yogananda

Anam Cara or *Eternal Echoes,* John O'Donohue

The Naked Now or *Immortal Diamond,* Richard Rohr

The Holy Trinity and the Law of Three or *Mystical Hope,* Cynthia Bourgeault

Practicing the Presence or *The Infinite Way,* Joel Goldsmith

Love Is a Fire or *Fragments of a Love Story,* Llewellyn Vaughan-Lee

Gratefulness: The Heart of Prayer, Brother David Steindl-Rast

Black Elk Speaks, John G. Neihardt

Care of the Soul, Thomas Moore

Desert Wisdom or *The Sufi Book of Life,* Neil Douglas-Klotz

Entering the Castle, Caroline Myss

Breakthrough: Meister Eckhart's Creation Spirituality in New Translation, Matthew Fox

The Dark Night of the Soul, translation by Mirabai Starr

The Heart of Buddha's Teachings or *Living Buddha, Living Christ,* Thich Nhat Hanh

Discourses or *God Speaks,* Meher Baba

Tao Te Ching, translation by Jonathan Star or Stephen Mitchell

Poetry

Thirst and many others by Mary Oliver

House of Belonging or *Pilgrim* and others by David Whyte

The Essential Rumi and others, translated by Coleman Barks

Rumi Thief of Sleep, Shahram Shiva

Book of Hours, Rainer Maria Rilke

The Enlightened Heart: An Anthology of Sacred Poetry, Stephen Mitchell

Meditations with Meister Eckhart and other meditations by Matthew Fox

The Gift, Love Poems from God and others, translated by Daniel Ladinsky

The Conference of the Birds: A Sufi Fable by Farid ud-Din Attar; also consider the Peter Sis version with gorgeous drawings

Mother of God, Similar to Fire, icons by William Hart McNichols, reflections by Mirabai Starr (a lovely mix of *visio divina* and *lectio divina)*

Set Up Vibrant Spiritual Practices

Your soul vows will be the cornerstone of your daily spiritual practice. Speaking them aloud each day will infuse all your other prayers and practices with new levels of meaning and joy. So here, at the beginning of your soul vows adventure, is a good time to look at your current spiritual practices. Do you have any? Do you like them? Do you engage in them every day, or often, or only occasionally? Do you look forward to your spiritual practices, or do they feel like another thing on your to-do list? When you engage in your practices, do you come away refreshed or dry? Do your practices prepare you to embrace life, or do you feel sometimes that all you're doing is going through the motions? Do your practices feel like soul play or work? Do your current practices give you a taste, a hint, a whiff of who you really are—the beloved of the Divine?

Look at what you currently do and simply ponder these kinds of expansive questions. And please don't limit your definition of "spiritual practice" to time set aside for meditation, prayer, or deep soul writing. Spiritual practice includes your first thoughts in the morning and your last thoughts at night. It includes how you treat your work space, your home, your car. It includes how you prepare food and how you pay bills. It includes the words you speak to other people. And it surely includes the words you say to and about yourself.

An ideal place to do this kind of observation is on the page in deep soul writing. Your hand and heart know things your mind does not. So don't try to "think" your way to the "right" spiritual practices. Instead, simply look over your days, ask expansive questions, and allow your inner knowing to surface in your heart and on the page.

What are my current spiritual practices?

Do they feed me or does my heart long for something more?

What would a vibrant spiritual practice look like or sound like or feel like?

If you feel a desire to embrace some new spiritual practices or expand the ones you have, the following are a few ideas your soul might enjoy.

DON'T JUST SAY YOUR PRAYERS, BE YOUR PRAYERS

I love prayer. I love thinking about prayer. I love reading about prayer. I love embracing the prayer traditions of others. I love the sound and feel of prayers in other languages and other times in my mouth. I've always thought of prayer as words—beautiful and powerful words, perhaps—but still words. Prayer had much to teach me about the deeper nature of prayer.

In 2013, a federal judge sent my son, Jerry, to prison to coerce him to name his fellow political activists in front of a secret grand jury. All the words of all the prayers I knew suddenly turned to ash in my mouth. Never have I felt so unable to pray. I crawled off to St. Michael's Shrine in Tarpon Springs, Florida, plopped myself down in front of the huge hammered silver icon of St. Michael destroying the demon, and begged for help. Without thinking, I asked in my soul-writing journal, "How would a mystic pray for Jerry?"

This is what poured onto the page:

> The Divine in me, through me, and as me
> Blesses my precious son, Jerry,
> Honors his soul's divinely appointed mission,
> And showers him with grace.

This prayer felt alive and so true and holy. The first thing I loved about it is that it doesn't ask for anything. I am so weary of the popular mode of praying that reminds God what you need and then has the audacity to tell the Divine how you want your life to look. It would be funny if it weren't so sad. We have transformed our relationship with the mystery into a machine we think we can poke and prod to dispense what we want when we want it. My heart thumped in joy at this simple prayer that puts my hand where it belongs—in God's hand—and promises to share in the task of blessing and showering the world with grace.

This prayer felt perfect—so much so, that I called it "the Perfect Prayer." I was hungry to bring it to life. I went home and pulled out a stone necklace a friend had given me from El Camino de Santiago, the ancient pilgrimage road from Véze-lay, France, to Santiago de Compostela in Spain. The stone has a scallop shell, the symbol of St. James and of the pilgrimage, carved on the front. I resolved to wear it every day my son was in prison. Every morning as I put it on, I said the Perfect Prayer, and every evening as I took it off, I said the prayer again. And in between, whenever I worried about Jerry, I clenched the stone and said the prayer again. Sometimes, when I couldn't speak, I simply pressed the stone to my heart. As the days progressed, the stone changed from light gray to dark gray to dark brown. The stone itself became a prayer.

After five months in federal prison, Jerry began to suffer greatly. Nothing seemed to give him any comfort. I turned to the Masters and Teachers of the Akashic Record through Lauralyn Bunn and begged them to teach me how to help my son. They said to call together a critical mass of people and invite them to look at a photograph of the prison at the same time every day and for five minutes shower the prison with divine love and light. That was it. No words. No intention. Not even the desire to speed up Jerry's release. Just shower the prison and everyone connected with it with divine love and light.

A minister who joined the circle said she thought these five minutes of pure love and light might be "the Ultimate Prayer." Several members of the circle said this was the most powerful practice they'd ever experienced.

One morning, I glanced at the clock and realized it was almost time to pray. I stood up and said out loud, "It's time to go be the prayer." I heard myself and laughed. *Oh!* Don't *say* the prayer, *be* the prayer!

Thanks to the Ultimate Prayer, I now know that prayers do not have to have words. And even prayers that do have words, like the Perfect Prayer or our soul vows, are meant not to be a series of words, but to *be* the presence of light and love in the world. So whatever prayers you choose, don't just say them, *be* them!

What does be the prayer mean to me?

Have I ever had the experience of being a prayer?

How can I shift from saying my prayers to being my prayers?

ALTER YOUR SPACE WITH AN ALTAR

Do you have an altar in your home? Even if you think you don't, you probably do. It might be a niche with your grandmother's favorite statue in it, or a row of family photos on your mantel, or a few special things gathered on your nightstand. Altars matter. They have held an essential place in humanity's spiritual life from the most ancient times to the present.

An altar shifts your attention and alters the space. Is it an accident that the noun *altar* and the verb *alter* sound exactly the same? I don't think so. Here's how I remember which is which. The *a* in *altar* tells me *how* to create sacred space: put *a thing* down in a special place. What thing? Any thing that feels important or holy or special, any thing that lifts my spirit or reminds me of the mystery of life. The *e* in *alter* reminds me why sacred space matters: each thing on my altar emanates *energy*, and that energy literally changes my space.

When you have your soul vows in a few weeks, you will put them in a place where they can feed you. Because they are so holy, the spot where you place your soul vows will automatically become sacred space. My soul vows hang over my creative altar in my office. It's just the top shelf of a low bookcase; what makes it an altar are the things I put on it and what they mean to me. Everything on my altar is a treasure that feeds my soul and supports me in my holy work. The dried dragonfly kindly died on my doorstep while I was writing *Writing Down Your Soul*; I took it as a sacred sign from the writing gods and gave it a permanent place on my altar. The Canadian nickel rolled in front of my feet in the grocery store the day I got my divine marching orders, "Your soul wants five things."

When my son was sent to prison, I cleared off a large round end table in the living room and created an altar of freedom for him. I wanted to do something special to honor his willingness to sacrifice himself to protect our right to dissent. The first thing I put on it was a large, rather flat ceramic bowl I had bought years ago. Then I got out a box of small river rocks for floral arrangements that I'd never used. Each morning, I took out a rock, wrote the date on one side in permanent marker and the number of days Jerry had been in prison on the other side. As I placed each day's rock in the bowl I said the Perfect Prayer with my whole heart and my whole body, moving my hands over the bowl in vertical line, a horizontal line, and finally a full circle.

As people heard about Jerry's imprisonment, they sent gifts for his altar: a statue of the Hindu god Ganesh (the remover of obstacles), a hand-carved angel from Nicaragua, a prayer wheel made out of bike spokes, and a crocheted star sent all the way from Switzerland. I later placed a white statue of the Ascended Christ behind the bowl, and on the tenth anniversary of his father's death, I placed Jerry's father's ashes beside the bowl too. From then on, when I prayed the Perfect Prayer over the bowl, I felt that all the beings on the altar—Christ, Jerry's father, the angels, Ganesh—were saying the prayer with me. When we showered Jerry with grace, he was showered!

Is there something you wish to commemorate? Someone you want to pray for? A purpose you wish to bless? Wander around your home and gather a few things and create your altar. You needn't spend any money. You can if you want to, but you can also simply ask the universe to provide you with the perfect gifts. The first time I carried my shattered heart out for a long walk on the Pinellas Trail after Jerry was sent to prison, a perfect four-inch dark brown feather drifted to my feet. I carried it home to take its place at the top of the rocks in Jerry's bowl of freedom.

What spaces in my home or office are already altars?

Where do I want to create a sanctified altar space?

What is the purpose or intention of my altar?

What belongs on it?

How will I use my altar every day?

TAKE A SACRED REST

In the biblical story of creation, God spoke the world into existence for six days and then exhaled and rested on the seventh. But we humans, with our endless to-do lists and bottomless sense of self-importance, keep ourselves in full go-mode all day long, all week long, all year long. And then, we wonder why we're weary right down to our souls. I think God had it right; take a rest, already!

In that day or half day or even two-hour space of nothingness, your body will find respite, and your spirit will be refreshed in the mystery. Rest isn't a spiritual obligation; it's how we are wired. We are made to go and then stop. Our daily cycle of wakefulness followed by sleep is a clue. Look at the world. Night follows day. Winter follows fall. But we ignore our natural cycles. The price for this neglect is burnout and exhaustion.

In the Jewish tradition, as the sun sets on Friday night, the family stops what they're doing, gathers around Shabbat candles, says prayers, sings songs, reads Torah, shares a lovely meal, and enters into a full day of rest. Think about it. When was the last time you gave yourself a whole day of rest? Can you even remember? Keep in mind that "rest" doesn't mean shopping or cleaning out the closets or taking the kids to an amusement park. Rest means doing what the Creator did on the seventh day—nothing. When was the last time you gave yourself a block of time with nowhere to go and nothing to do?

I did this a couple years ago when Jennifer Hill Robenalt, my heaven-sent publicist, yelled at me to shut off the computer and stay out of the office for five days. I couldn't imagine how in the world I could do that. What about all the emails left unanswered? What about all the marketing opportunities I'd miss? But I did it. I turned off the computer, locked the door to my office, and spent five days reading, praying, and soul writing. I sat in the garden. I went for long, slow walks. I slept for ten, eleven, twelve hours. I made myself delicious meals and set the table with my best linens and crystal. I didn't talk to anyone or go anywhere, and I didn't accomplish a single thing. At the end of five days, I didn't want to open the office, so I gave myself two more days of complete solitude and rest. On the morning of the eighth day, I turned on my computer. There were twenty-two invitations to speak and teach, and I had not created, or asked for, or chased a single one of them.

Don't wait till you need a whole week of rest. Take one day—starting now. You might just want to make it a habit.

When was the last time I gave myself a total time off?

How can I incorporate a Sabbath into my life?

When am I going to start?

DON'T GET OUT OF BED SO FAST

There is one fairly unusual thing I do that feels like the special sauce in my spiritual and writing life: I do not get out of bed in the morning. Instead, as I'm slowly returning from the night world, I lie perfectly still. I do not open my eyes. I do not turn my head or lift it off the pillow. And in those theta-drenched, not-yet-awake moments, I receive words and images I could never conjure on my own. This is how I hear the titles of all my books. This is how I get topics for my newsletters. This is how I heard the name of my radio show, *The Soul-Directed Life.* And of course, I was lying in bed the morning I heard, "Your soul wants five things."

You already know how to slip into theta in your deep soul writing, so you'll find it easy to stretch your time in theta in the morning. Simply lie still as your brain comes up from the slowest delta brain waves of sleep and passes into theta. If you leap out of bed the moment your alarm goes off, you leave all the beautiful possibilities that could have happened in theta on the pillow. Is lollygagging in bed a vibrant spiritual practice? Absolutely! And it's one of my favorites.

Have I had an experience of waking in the morning knowing something?

How can I change my mornings to create a pocket of time in theta?

FIND THE HOLY IN THE HORRIBLE

Watching my son suffer in prison triggered a depth of spiritual practice I didn't know existed. Like Alice tumbling into a world where the standard rules of physics no longer applied, I found myself in a world where the standard rules of spiritual practice didn't seem to apply. Nothing was working. Nothing fed me. Nothing could even hold my attention. I realized there's only one thing that can carry us through tragedy, and that one thing is trust. So I followed where I was led.

Eventually, I was led to the hardscrabble ground of the richest spiritual practice of all: forgiveness. Now, I've had a little experience with forgiveness. If you've read *Writing Down Your Soul*, you know that after three years of intense deep soul writing, the day came when I forgave my ex-husband with every cell of my being, and a miracle ensued. After that, I forgave the judge who had thwarted me at every turn during our divorce.

But with forgiveness, there's always more to learn. That more came to me when I realized I had to forgive the federal judge who had sent my son to prison—and not *after* he let my son out. I was being called to forgive the judge *while* my son was still in prison. This was much harder than forgiving my ex-husband or our divorce judge after our battles had ended. Suddenly Jesus' radical teaching "Love your enemies, do good to those who hate you" (Luke 6:27) was real, and it was in my face.

The federal judge's face floated forward in my mind, and I said out loud, "God loves Judge _____ as much as God loves me." Now, I know that truth may sound obvious to you, but for me, at that moment, it was a revelation—perhaps *the* revelation. It was a revelation that no one is other—no one, no matter who they are or what they've done, is withheld from the heart of the Divine. This was it. This was the opening, the calling, the moment when I had to—*had to*—forgive that judge and bless him and pray for him and make room for him in my heart, even as my son was suffering. This was my moment to "love my enemy."

I gripped my Camino stone necklace harder than I'd ever gripped it before and spoke the Perfect Prayer for the judge. I choked the first time, so I made myself say it again. And again. And again. I said it until I believed it:

> The Divine in me, through me, and as me,
> Blesses Judge _____,
> Honors his soul's divinely appointed mission,
> And showers him with grace.

Do you see why forgiveness belongs here under "vibrant spiritual practices"? In fact, it may be the most living, breathing, essential practice of all. But it's the one we turn away from, isn't it? Meditation? Sure! Ritual? You bet! Contemplation? Absolutely! Forgive your enemies? Uh, maybe not.

If you're willing, call up a picture of a person who was a source of misery and suffering in your life. See the person's face before you. Take a deep breath. Take another. Then speak the truth out loud: "God loves _____ as much as God loves me."

Now stop. Don't do a thing. Just let that truth sink in. That may be enough for now. But when you're ready—when your soul cries out to be free of anger and resentment, judgment and pain, when your soul begs to find the holy in the horrible—forgive that person, and forgive with all your heart.

When will that be? I can't tell you. No one can. It's only you who can—and will—recognize the moment, and it may be a most ordinary moment. But you'll know in your heart, "This is it; this is my invitation to love my enemy." And when you do, you may discover the head-scratching paradox Thich Nhat Hanh lays out for us in *Living Buddha, Living Christ*: "To 'love our enemy' is impossible because the moment we love him, he is no longer our enemy."

How will you forgive? If the Perfect Prayer helps, take it; it's yours. Or, if you are in pain right now, consider how Jesus forgave. In the midst of being tortured to death, he called out, not in anger but in forgiveness. But—and I think this is very important—Jesus didn't do the forgiving. He asked *his Father* to do the forgiving. Perhaps it isn't we who forgive at all. Forgiveness sweeps both the forgiven and the forgiver on a warm tsunami of love all the way to a blessed state of wholeness. Who or what can do that but the mystery?

Jesus said, "Father, forgive them; they know not what they do" (Luke 23:34). When I applied these words to the federal judge, forgiveness suddenly became possible, doable, almost easy. In my mouth it came out,

Oh, Father-Mother God, source of all life, hear me.

This one prays. This one prays not for me, but for another.

Oh, Father-Mother God, forgive Judge _____

for he knows not what he does.

And then, I gave the gift of forgiveness to myself: "Oh Father-Mother God, forgive me for I know not what I do."

I had to sit with that one a long time.

How will you forgive? Ask for guidance and trust that you will be led to a vibrant forgiveness practice of your own. The important thing is to *do* it. Do it every day. Do it until forgiveness is your friend. Do it until you become forgiveness and forgiveness becomes you. If our purpose in soul vows is to *be* the presence of the Divine in us, through us, and as us, then surely we are called to do what the Divine does best—forgive. We may not do anything more important.

Who am I being called to forgive?

How shall I forgive?

CREATE YOUR DESERT CAVE OF SOLITUDE

Everything we need to know about the critical importance of solitude is in *The Way of the Heart,* a slip of a book by the prolific and saintly Henri Nouwen. In less than a hundred pages, he distills the priceless wisdom of the desert fathers and mothers, who retired to the Egyptian desert in the fourth and fifth centuries to find deeper communion with the Divine. The book has just three chapters: "Solitude," "Silence," and "Prayer." I'll let Nouwen tell you why solitude comes first: "Solitude is the furnace of transformation. Without solitude we remain victims of our society and continue to be entangled in the illusions of the false self."

So how can we begin? How can we create a desert of solitude smack in the middle of our crazy, busy, over-booked, overstimulated lives? How can we heed the call of the desert fathers and mothers and become best friends with solitude and silence in a world that positively loathes both?

Start with the realization that we are *not* as needed as we think we are. It is we who create the expectation that we must respond to everyone and everything. It's we who keep ourselves in constant reaction mode at work, at home, with friends. Even when we are physically apart, we stay in relentless reaction mode through online and media contact. So when we finally have a chance to be alone, we make sure we're not alone. Why do we do this to ourselves? We do it because constant reaction keeps our focus *outside* ourselves. And staying busy is the world's most honorable and admirable method to avoid going *inside* to wrestle with the real meaning of life. But the soul is hungry. As Thomas Moore reminds us in *Care of the Soul*, "Spirituality does demand attention, mindfulness, regularity, and devotion. It asks for some small measure of withdrawal from a world set up to ignore soul."

So begin small. All you need is a little time and a little space. Set aside fifteen or twenty minutes and go to the quietest room in your house. And it needn't be a whole room. It could be a chair, a desk, a pillow. Nor does it have to be in your house. I know a woman whose sacred space is a bench in the park, another who slips out to her car during her morning break, and a man who locks his office door at lunch for thirty minutes. A woman in Connecticut sits on her living room sofa and opens a beautiful box containing her journal, pen, a book of mystical poetry, a tiny statue, a gold ribbon, and a small rock that are dear to her—everything she needs for her cave of solitude. After struggling to be consistent in her spiritual practice, a friend in New Mexico set up a recurring message on her cell phone with a special ring tone. Every morning, she receives a text from God: "Good morning, sweetheart. I am waiting for you in our Blue Room."

Everyone fashions his or her own desert cave, but here are a few suggestions to help you create a sacred container of solitude.

Intend. As you step over the threshold into the space, set the intention to withdraw from the world and be alone with the Divine for a window of time. This may be the matter of a moment, a thought, a tap of the heart, a breath, but it marks the place where you are as holy. To help you remember, you might put a picture or word or talisman at the entrance to your space. Then, as you look at it or touch it, you will be reminded of your purpose in entering your cave.

Invoke. As you settle, say a short phrase that creates a welcoming space for divine Presence. I call it an invocation because I love the word, but please don't think you are inviting God to join you from somewhere in space; quite the opposite. As Meister Eckhart said in his pithy way, "God is at home. We are the ones who have gone out for a walk." So your invocation is more of a "Honey, I'm home" call from the door of your heart.

My favorite invocation is *Hineni*—"Here I am." This is how Abraham answered each time Yahweh called his name in Genesis. It means more than "I am physically here"; it means "I am open, I am listening, I am ready, I am present, I am yours." I love speaking an invocation in another language because it helps me slip out of conscious mind and into sacred mind.

Here are a few other invocations you might love. In Aramaic, Jesus said *Abwoon,* which is translated "Our Father," but according to Neil Douglas-Klotz means something closer to "Oh Breathing Life." Another lovely practice is to speak one of the ninety-nine names of God each time you enter your cave. You can find the phonetic Arabic pronunciation, along with a short heart meditation, at the end of each of the ninety-nine chapters in Douglas-Klotz's *The Sufi Book of Life*. Or perhaps you'd like to intone the ancient Arabic sacred formula: *La ilaha illa-Allah*—"there is no god but One God." This is the most revered invocation in all of Islam. It has the same heart resonance as the most holy prayer in the Jewish tradition: *Sh'ma Yisrael Adonai Elohaynnu Adonai Ehad*—"Hear, O Israel, the Lord our God, the Lord is One."

In the Vedic tradition, the Sanskrit mantra for opening sacred space invokes Ganesh, the epitome of auspiciousness and the remover of obstacles: *Om gam Ganpatiyei namaha*. It means "Om! My deepest salutations to Lord Ganesh."

Of course, you can invoke divine Presence in English, too. I heard Ron Roth in Tampa once, and his invocation was short and powerful: *Come, Holy Spirit, come.* Everyone in the sanctuary that day felt holy presence. Thich Nhat Hanh recommends this beautiful short invocation: *I have arrived, I am home, in the here and in the now. I am solid, I am free, in the ultimate I dwell.* When I say this poem with my whole heart, I am transformed. Go inside and find your own sweet invocation.

Shift. Because we are such creatures of doing, a transition of some kind helps us gather our attention away from the outside and focus it gently on the inside. It's like shifting a speeding car to a lower gear to slow down. You might take a few deep breaths, then speak a prayer or read a passage from a sacred text, or from your master-companion book, or from a poem by a mystic. Or you might listen to a short meditation or sacred chant. You might sing a hymn or song that reminds you of your purpose. I love the opening stanza of Daniel Nahmod's *Inside (To Find My God)* so much I asked him if it could be the theme song for *The Soul-Directed Life* radio show: "I will leave the world as it is; go inside to find my God."

Here's how I downshift: I stand barefoot on my prayer rug, take a few deep breaths, light a sacred candle, and ask the voice of the Tibetan bowl to call me to listen. When I'm upset and need more help settling down, I hold *The Gift* or other book of mystical poetry to my heart and ask for help. The poem I open to always pulls me away from my worries and into my heart. There's great comfort in a set ritual, but be open and responsive to the call of your heart for what it needs in the moment.

Be. For this little window of time, all you have to do is be— be quiet, be still, be present, be open, be gentle, be with yourself, and be with your God. If you wish to meditate, be that. Do you love Centering Prayer? Be that. If you want to close your eyes and just sit there, be that. If you want to gaze at a sacred image, be that. I love to sit in my chair and soul write, but sometimes I look up and stare across the room at a beautiful Greek icon painting of Archangels Michael and Gabriel. I can't explain what happens, but as I look into their eyes I feel comforted and fed.

Thank. A perfect way to close your time in your desert cave is to say thank you. We say thank you so often in our daily lives that we no longer hear ourselves. The phrase, however, has profound meaning. In *Gratefulness, the Heart of Prayer,* Brother David Steindl-Rast reminds us, "The greatest gift we one can give is thanksgiving. In giving gifts, we give what we can spare, but in giving thanks we give ourselves. One who says 'Thank you' to another really says, 'We belong together.'" Just think, when you say "Thank you" to the Beloved, you are saying, "We belong together." Really, can you think of a more beautiful prayer? That must be why Meister Eckhart said, "If the only prayer you ever say in your entire life is thank you, it will be enough." So whether you perceived anything or not, felt anything or not, heard anything or not, say thank you because you have been held in the heart of the Beloved, and now you belong together.

Carry. Your visit to your cave of solitude may be ending, but its gifts are just beginning. The key is to carry the desert with you. Put a grain of divine sand in your pocket and head back to the world.

Of course, the world will do what it does so well—yank you right back into commotion and worry and fear. So I find repeating a short phrase or mantra helps me remember the truth that's in my pocket. My favorite came from a peregrine falcon who sat on a telephone wire a few feet from my front door a couple years ago. I had never seen a peregrine falcon before, and I sensed his presence was important. I sat beneath him and asked for his blessing. Thanks to falcon, my grain-of-sand mantra is "You carry me." No matter what's happening, when I whisper these words, I feel myself on the back of my falcon angel, and I remember again that Spirit carries me, and always has, and always will.

While you're in the cave, ask your Beloved for a little grain to put in your pocket. It may be a word, a phrase, an image, a color. Or it may be something tangible, like a little stone or medal. Then carry the Divine with you wherever you go.

What will happen in your cave of solitude? Will it turn out to be a "furnace of transformation" for you? Will it prevent you from becoming a "victim of society?" I think so. There is a reason every spiritual tradition insists we go inside and spend time alone with Source.

Henri Nouwen tells us we have to "fashion our own desert where we can withdraw every day, shake off our compulsions, and dwell in the gentle healing presence of our Lord"; he doesn't tell us exactly how. That is a sweet exploration between you and the Divine. All I can suggest is that you create a cave of solitude and enter it regularly. Over time I think you will discover that what happens in this sacred container is more precious and important than anything that happens outside. Or as Henri Nouwen says, "Solitude is not simply a means to an end. Solitude is its own end."

What and where is my cave of solitude?

When and how shall I enter it?

Am I ready for the transformation that can happen there?

First Paradox: I Am Human; I Am Divine

What have you learned about yourself and your true lineage in this first-chakra exploration? This chakra is called the root chakra because its Sanskrit name, *Muladhara,* means "root support." Hearing the word *root,* we tend to visualize roots like plant roots flowing down our legs, grounding us to our physical place on earth and to our biological heritage. But there's also something more happening in this first chakra. "Muladhara Chakra is the seat of the coiled Kundalini and is the root of all growth and awareness of human divinity," says Harish Johari in *Chakras: Energy Centers of Transformation.*

Human divinity—that's what this first exploration has been about, and that's the first great paradox in soul vows. In the yogic tradition, Shakti, often called Kundalini, is the divine feminine energy of creation. It is her cry for her Beloved that sparks the spiritual journey back to the One. We are looking through the lens of a Vedic system, but this cry is universal. Mystics of all traditions speak of it. In *Fragments of a Love Story*, Llewellyn Vaughan-Lee, a profound Sufi author, describes it this way:

> The soul's primal cry of separation ignites our secret passion for union with God. This great love affair begins with this cry, a love affair that will tear apart every thread of our being and draw us from the separation of the ego to the union of the Self.

This sounds so familiar to me. I can look back now and see that my cry "I want You to find me!" was the cry of my soul, my Shakti, my Kundalini, for union with the Beloved. In the chakra system, Kundalini is depicted as a coiled snake at the base of the root chakra. As she is awakened by prayer, desire, grace, or by a teacher, Shakti slowly rises through the subtle energy chakras up the spine all the way to the seventh chakra, where she unites with Shiva, the divine masculine energy of limitless potential. When they unite, all is united—lover and Beloved, feminine and masculine, heaven and earth, human and divine.

Meister Eckhart, the great Christian mystic, describes our dual lineage this way:

> Every human person is an aristocrat,
> every human person is noble and of royal blood.
> Who is more noble than someone who is born,
> on the one hand,
> from the highest and best that a creature possesses
> and who, on the other hand,
> is born
> from the intimate depths of the divine nature
> and the divine wilderness?
>
> *Meditations with Meister Eckhart,* Matthew Fox

Use the triangle below to capture how the paradox of the two apparent opposites of your dual human-divine lineage generate a third holy truth. On my triangle, I put the sentences "I am human" on one side and "I am divine" on the other to describe how I perceive the paradox of this first chakra. But please use your own wording. Perhaps you like the ancient god and goddess images of Shiva and Shakti, or some version of Meister Eckhart's aristocratic lineages. On the dotted line across the bottom, record the new revelation of the union of these two apparent opposites. For me, that's "I am an embodied soul."

Then, in the center space, draw an image that captures the essence of this new awareness. For me, a lovely image of the divine human is the sacred heart. I grew up with a large painting of Jesus with a glowing red heart in the entrance to my childhood home. I forgot about that image until I went to Oaxaca, Mexico four years ago. In every hotel room, restaurant, and home we entered, there was a large, red and gold metal sacred heart on the wall. At first, it was disconcerting, but by the time I left Oaxaca, I wanted a sacred heart on my wall at home. But Jesus is not the only one with a sacred heart; each one of us has a sacred heart. Each one of us is a divine human.

Go inside and ask your soul for an image that captures your personal revelation of the divine human. It might be a head with a halo, a sun and moon, or a tree with roots deep in the earth and branches high in the heavens. Or perhaps you'd like to honor the classic chakra story by drawing a rising Kundalini Shakti serpent. It needn't be a picture; the colors red and purple for the first and seventh chakras might be a lovely symbol of your dual lineage. Whatever image you choose to symbolize your dual lineage, put it in the center of your triangle.

I'm showing you my first chakra triangle, just to show you how it might look, but please don't copy mine. It's more fun and much more meaningful to capture your own exploration of the paradox of the divine human. If you want more room, draw a larger triangle in your journal or an even bigger one on a full size piece of paper.

I am human

I am Divine

I am an embodied soul

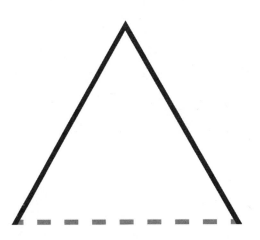

First Discovery: I Am Ready

After your adventures in this first exploration, I'll bet you have a new understanding and deeper appreciation of the words that welcomed you to this chapter: "Once the soul awakens, the search begins . . . you are inflamed with a special longing that will never again let you linger in the lowlands of complacency and partial fulfillment. The eternal makes you urgent."

That sounds like Shakti surging upward through the chakras to her beloved Shiva, doesn't it? And it reminds me of my cry, "I want You to find me!" Are John O'Donohue's words now true for you, too? Has your soul grabbed your attention and won't let you go? Do you feel a special longing whether you can define what it is or not? Is a life of complacency simply no longer acceptable? Is a life that is only partially fulfilled no longer enough? Is something urgent bubbling up inside?

If so, then you're ready. That's the first discovery, and it's just that simple. "I am ready." I am ready to embrace my dual lineage and get to know my royal Self. I am ready for the fullness of life. I am ready to grow toward my godhood. I am ready to become the divine human I am here to be. I am ready to unite Shiva and Shakti, heaven and earth. I am ready to be one with the One.

Say it in your own words, but say it. Say it out loud. Say it in your cave of solitude. Say it in your daily prayers. Say it as you're falling asleep. Say it as you wake. "I am ready" is a powerful prayer. It sets everything in motion and propels you onward to the next exploration in soul vows. Put "I am ready" in your pocket and carry it with you to your next exploration.

Second Exploration

recognize the false unconscious vows that have kept you fragmented

Second Chakra: Sacral Chakra
Second Paradox: My foe is my friend.
Second Discovery: I am free.

Whatever commands our attention is our master; whatever we worship consciously or unconsciously is what we serve.

Kabir Helminski, *Living Presence*

If you are driven by needs and inner forces of which you are unaware, then your behavior and actions are not free; you only partly belong to yourself. To bring these subtle forces into the light helps change their negative control over you.

John O'Donohue, *Eternal Echoes*

In your first-chakra exploration, you felt the simultaneous downward energy of your human roots and the upward energy of your divine heritage, and discovered you are ready to embrace both. With your "I am ready" talisman in your pocket, you are ready for your deep soul exploration of the second chakra. Here, the false will reveal the true hiding inside, and the broken will lead you to wholeness.

You will identify the false beliefs and habits that have held dominion over you and notice how they have kept you fragmented, distracted, and afraid. You will create a safe space to call your shadows forward, invite them to sit down, and listen as they tell their stories and reveal the gifts they've been trying to give you. As you get to know and befriend your shadows, you will gather yourself back into your natural state of wholeness. In that refreshed state of wholeness, your new and glorious vows can and will make themselves known. But before you can get clear about the vows you *want to live,* it's necessary to look at the vows you are *already living.*

The truth is, you're already living a big pile of vows—and you might not like a lot of them. Every time you repeat a fear-based thought, whether you are conscious of it or not, you are "vowing" to live that fear and reinforcing its presence and its power in your life. Not consciously reinforcing it, perhaps, but energetically that is what is happening. And it is reinforced in your physical brain, as well. Perhaps you've heard the phrase "what fires together, wires together." That's brain science. Every time you repeat an automatic, ingrained, fear-based response, you carve that unwanted neural programming a little deeper into your brain. After decades of thoughts and feelings of doubt, unworthiness, distrust— whatever your false vows may be—being repeated over and over again, those neural programs are deeply entrenched. And those entrenched patterns have real power over your thoughts, your view of the world, your emotions, and your behavior.

Mahatma Gandhi wasn't a brain scientist, but he completely understood what happens as our neural pathways get carved deeper and deeper:

> *Your beliefs become your thoughts.*
> *Your thoughts become your words.*
> *Your words become your actions.*
> *Your actions become your habits.*
> *Your habits become your values.*
> *Your values become your destiny.*

Kabir Helminski condenses Gandhi's formula into one line in *Living Presence*: "What we love we will become." We like to think that the word *love* applies only to beautiful things, but when you repeat *any* feeling or thought, you are "loving" it—that is, you are giving it room and honor and attention in your heart and your mind. And slowly, over time, without realizing it, a falsehood becomes your master.

Here's a comparison of two masters: the false vows you have been living unconsciously and the beautiful soul vows your heart is waiting to give you.

False Unconscious Vows	Soul Vows
Qualities of personality or ego	Qualities of the Divine
Keep you contracted	Keep you expanded
Leave you fragmented	Lead to wholeness
Not your authentic self	Your authentic self
Not aligned with your soul's purpose	Aligned with your soul's purpose
Generated in response to frightening or stress-filled human situations	Generated from the soul
Energized by fear	Energized by love
Produce a sense of duality	Create unity
Response to external forces	Response to internal truths
Feel separated and alone	Experience divine communion
Path of control (attempted control)	Path of surrender
Reactive	Proactive
Unconscious, automatic response	Conscious choice
Go through life asleep	Live wide awake

Your soul's desire is to declare and live vows that have all these beautiful qualities and radiate divine Presence. As you "love" your soul vows with daily repetition and commitment, you will develop new and very beautiful neural pathways in your brain, and their creative power will influence your thoughts, words, actions, habits, values, and destiny. Over time you will *become* your soul vows. But before you can declare your beautiful soul vows, you need to stop for a moment and call up the false ones that are already there, already taking up energetic and physical space, and already exerting mastery over your life.

This conversation with your false masters takes place in the second chakra because the second chakra is the seat of your vast creative energy. Look at where the second chakra is located on the body; it's the womb. Male or female, we all have wombs where we gestate our lives. My three primary references on the chakras explore this creative capacity from different angles. Woven together, these three views of the second chakra create a powerful tapestry.

In *Anatomy of the Spirit,* Caroline Myss calls the second chakra the partnership chakra and talks about how its energy "enables us to generate a sense of personal identity and protective psychological boundaries." She emphasizes that the second chakra is the chakra of choice: "Managing the power of choice, with all its creative and spiritual implications, is *the essence of the human experience*" (her italics). As you become a wiser custodian of your power of choice in this exploration, you prepare yourself to make a very conscious choice to embody divine Presence through your soul vows. Until now, choice may have been a hidden and reactive undercurrent, but as you become conscious of your power to create, choice will become a visible, active, and beloved partner.

In *Wheels of Life,* Anoeda Judith says that the second chakra is the energy of change, but change can only occur when we become aware of differences. "Consciousness . . . is stimulated by the dance of polarities," she explains. "In the upper chakras we reach levels of consciousness that transcend dualism, but in the second chakra, duality becomes the motivating force for movement and change." That sounds like the creative tension of wrestling with paradox, doesn't it?

In the classically oriented *Chakras: Energy Centers of Transformation*, Harish Johari translates the second chakra's Sanskrit name, *Svadhishthana*, as "Dwelling Place of the Self." The doorkeeper of the second chakra is depicted as an aspect of Kundalini-Shakti, with two heads indicating the duality of the I and the other, the inner world and the outer world. By the time you're finished here, you will have found the wholeness in that tension of opposites, but first you have to see them, learn from them, and choose your masters.

Reading about what happens in this chakra, you might be tempted to skip all this exploration of the under-conscious and jump into the fourth chakra, the heart chakra, and start calling in your beautiful vows. Please don't. If you bypass this second-chakra experience of getting to know your false, unconscious vows, and the third-chakra experience of releasing them, the first time you try to say your beautiful new soul vows, your old negative neural programming will hear you affirm a vow that is sweet and positive and holy, and it will have a nice little chuckle, roll its eyes, and spit out, "Oh, puh-lease! Who do you think you're kidding?" You know that doubting voice. You know it all too well. It says things like, "Who do you think you are? You're not good enough. That'll never happen." For your beautiful vows to flourish, it's necessary to silence that critical voice.

But you can't silence your critical voice by yelling at it, or telling it to shut up, or ignoring it, or going to war with it. Instead, you're going to do the opposite; you're going to create a space in which all your critical voices can come forward, speak, and be heard. Sound counterintuitive? It is. It's just one more paradox on your journey into communion with the One.

Deep Soul Explorations

In this second deep soul exploration in the second chakra, you will:

recognize the false unconscious vows that have kept you fragmented   57

- create a welcoming space
- invite your critical voices to come forward
- notice how your false vows drain your power and keep you fragmented
- ask for and receive the gifts of your false vows
- identify what you want to release and make the decision to release

Create a Welcoming Space

Whether you know it or not, you've been avoiding a conversation with your critical voices for years. But avoiding and ignoring hasn't kept them silent, has it? Unbidden, they still show up in disturbing dreams, waves of self-doubt, and irrational outbursts that leave you surprised and embarrassed. Every time you sabotage yourself, rest assured one of your critical voices is in the background, mumbling words of doubt or shame or fear.

Your internal critics may not have been the kindest of companions, but they are still very important ones. They have much to share with you and much to teach you about your power of choice and what happens when you choose differently. As you listen to them and learn from them, you will reclaim your creative power and begin to use it wisely and for great good.

This may be your first friendly conversation with your internal critics, so begin by creating an open, nonjudgmental, receptive space in which you feel comfortable inviting them to come forward and they feel comfortable speaking. Here are a few thoughts on how to create receptive space.

Surround Yourself with Guides and Protection

Enter your cave of solitude. In that quiet place of gentle communion, call on your guides and guardians to stand beside you throughout this rich adventure. Do you know who your guides are? If you feel an affinity toward any angels, divine emanations, masters, or saints, call them by name and ask them to be with you.

When you call on a guide or teacher, something special happens when you call their name three times. It is another experience of the magical power of three. The first time you speak a teacher's name, you are saying "I honor you and wish to receive your wisdom." Then, as you speak their name a second time, you are saying, "I am open to receiving what you have to teach me." As you speak their name one last time, you are energetically absorbing their wisdom and integrating it into your being. Once you become aware of this power of three, you'll find yourself wanting to pray in sets of three all the time.

Your guides need not be personages. Perhaps you feel drawn to a sacred geometry symbol or an animal messenger or a color. If you're uncertain who or what is helping you, ask in deep soul writing, ask out loud as you go through your day, or ask as you are falling asleep. Then simply pay attention. An animal might cross your path or come to you in a dream. Your eye might be drawn to an image, your ear to a phrase or a song. And be sure to include your master-teacher companion in this quest. Reading a few pages in *lectio divina* may help you perceive what has been right in front of you all along.

With your guides beside you, speak a short prayer of protection. This is a lovely habit all the time, but especially as you converse with your internal critics. This particular prayer for protection has been said by millions since it was written by James Dillet Freeman for soldiers in World War II:

> The light of God surrounds me.
> The love of God enfolds me.
> The power of God protects me.
> The presence of God watches over me.
> Wherever I am, God is.

Or you might say the Perfect Prayer and change it to, "The Divine in me, through me, and as me blesses *my critical voices*, honors their divinely appointed mission, and showers them with grace." That shifts the energy totally from confrontation to blessing, doesn't it? Or write your own prayer of protection. Just enter into deep soul writing and ask your divine partner how to pray to create a safe sacred space in which to hear the wisdom of your internal critics.

Clarify Your Intention

What is your intention in calling forward your critical voices? I can't tell you what your individual intention *is*, but I can help you with what it is *not*. It is not to beat yourself up for the choices you've made. It is not to blame or punish yourself. It is not to blame or punish your internal critics, either. It isn't even to prove them wrong. All of that would be just another unsatisfying judging and blaming session with yourself, and you've had quite enough of that. Now you're ready to squeeze the good juice out of what appears on the surface to be negative.

So set your intention to meet your critics, hear them, and learn from them. You might surprise yourself and become friends in the process. Set your intention to honor the good they've done in your life and ask for their blessing. Set your intention to shift from feeling fragmented and distracted to gathered and whole. Say it however you want, but do set a holy intention for this important adventure.

Invite Your Critical Voices to Come Forward

With your guides beside you and a shawl of protection around you, you are ready to call your critics forward, one by one, and get to know them. The easiest way to do this is in deep soul writing. Your free-flowing, fast-moving, unediting hand can capture what they have to say more accurately and quickly than your mind can.

Just as you called on your guides three times, speak a welcome to your first critic three times. Does your critic have a name? If you're unsure, begin by making one up. Your critical voice keeps you fragmented, so *Fraggie* might work, or give it a sort-of-real-sounding name, like *Gertrudious* or *Hamstring*. Just don't give it the name of a real person in your life. It may turn out that one of your critical voices does sound like a parent or boss or ex-spouse, but don't predetermine that by giving your critic a specific person's name. You might give it a name that identifies what it does to you, like *Drain* or *Worry.* Alice in Illinois called her negative voice *Fraidy Kat* and shortened it to *Kat.* She had stunning conversations with "Dear Kat."

Invite your first critical voice to come forward and sit down. Smile, say hello, and thank it for coming. Start the conversation by telling your critical voice why you called it forward. Let it know you have no anger, no judgment; you just want to listen and understand. If it helps, visualize your critical voice sitting across from you. Is it wearing a mask? Critics typically do. They wear masks not to protect themselves, but to create camouflage that protects *you* from seeing what you have been unwilling to see. But you are ready. So ask your first critical voice to please take off its mask and show its face.

It may want to talk to you a bit before it's willing to do that. After all, you haven't been the kindest companion either. Thich Nhat Hanh's beautiful, caring practice "Beloved, I am here for you" can help you open the conversation. Calling your critic *Beloved* will soften your heart and leave you more open and receptive to hear what your critic has to tell you about the creative choices you've made.

When your critic does remove its mask, don't be surprised if it's not the ogre you expected. It may be a frightened child or confused teenager. Mine looked like a seven-year-old version of myself in a cotton dress with smocking across the chest, white anklets, and Mary Jane shoes. But your critic may not look like a person all. It may be an animal or a symbol or something unidentifiable. Whatever it looks like, gaze at it with love and tenderness. Your critical voice is not your enemy. The big "Aha!" here is realizing that your critic wasn't gripping you and pressuring you and forcing you to do anything. Quite the opposite. It was you who was clinging to it, thinking you needed it to be safe. Thank your first critic for showing up. Tell it you welcome its presence and its wisdom. Then ask it to tell you its story, which, of course, is your story.

Give Your Critic the Floor

Give your critic plenty of time and space to tell you what happened. Let it write for as long as it wants, telling you when and how your fear-based responses to life developed into hard-wired habits. Don't interrupt. Don't try to edit the story or explain your reactions or get your critic to change its mind about something. Just listen—and keep writing.

It may take several deep-soul-writing explorations to call up all your critics and their stories and dig through them to identify the powers, forces, and fears that have been a living presence in your life. You might begin looking at things that happened that were traumatic. For example, you might write about a teacher who humiliated you in front of the class, a friend you really liked who rejected you, or a minister who scolded you for asking questions. Here are a few deep-soul-writing questions that can help you get in touch with your stories. These are suggestions, not a checklist. I hope reading them will inspire you to allow the questions that want to bubble up from your soul to spill onto the page.

What are my biggest fears?

When did those fears begin?

Did something upsetting happen when I was little? How did my little self react?

What did my child self do to feel safe in that situation?

How have those little child beliefs continued to show up in my life?

What experiences shifted my view of life from safe to unsafe? Fun to hard work?

How did I change my behavior in response to those experiences?

When did I stop being self-confident and become fearful and self-doubting?

What fearful patterns do I see over and over again in my life?

Is there a story or belief that runs through all my relationships, homes, careers . . . ?

Slip into "We" and Ask Compassionate Questions

In this state of creative dialogue, you are pretending your critic is someone other than yourself. By giving it a name, asking it to come forward, and addressing it as *Beloved,* you seem to be speaking to someone other than yourself. But of course, your critic is not outside you; it is a habituated response you developed over time as you faced difficult and frightening situations. Those responses kept you safe—or seemed to at the time—but now, you are ready to understand those automatic unconscious responses and let them go. So let yourself slip into using the pronoun *we* while soul writing with each critical voice.

As the critic's story surfaces, you may feel a self-protective urge to justify your past behavior or get angry at your internal critic for being, well, your internal critic. But there's nothing to be learned if you blame or shame your critic or ask it what in the world it was thinking. On the other hand, there is much to be learned if you enter into compassionate dialogue. So ask it open-hearted, tender, compassionate questions. For example, as your critic is telling you a story, you might ask questions like:

How did we feel when that happened?

What did we do next?

Why do you think we reacted that way?

Did we see any other options at the time?

When do you think we began to look at the world that way?

How do we feel about this belief today?

What would we like to do now?

What do you want me to know?

Listen to What You Say Out Loud, Too

In addition to deep soul writing, listen to how you talk. Once you begin listening to yourself, you'll quickly recognize verbal habits that are generated by your internal critics.

Perhaps you'll hear yourself saying things "won't work" or are "too hard." You might catch yourself talking more about obstacles and problems than solutions and possibilities. Pay attention to the negative phrases that pop out of your mouth before you even think. Jot them down and notice how often and in how many different situations you use the same words to transfer blame or responsibility to another person or authority or situation or condition. Some triggers to listen for are *can't*, *need to* (as in "she needs to . . ."), or *wrong* (as in "what's wrong with these people?"). Or the one that makes everybody cringe: *should*. You probably have your own special triggers.

Pay attention to what you say when you slip into judgment of yourself and of others. Notice how often you remind yourself or others that life is hard, or you can't trust people, or there isn't enough, or any other habitual limiting assumption. And pay close attention to how often you steer yourself away from a divine impulse for a new idea or new experience and retreat back into familiar, no-risk territory. A few days of self-listening could be quite a revelation. Bring what you're learning about your spoken words onto the page and ask your critic to help you understand the verbal habits that keep you stuck.

Learn Your False Vows' Names

As you get to know the stories behind your various unconscious responses, you may find yourself starting to think of these patterns by a name or phrase. Just as your individual critics told you their names, took off their masks, revealed their faces, and began to talk, your false vows are now coming forward and revealing their names to help you understand your unconscious habitual responses to life.

A big one of mine, for example, was Obligation. In extended deep soul writing, I realized I'd been living under a very large false cloud laden with all the things I thought I *had* to do. Once I recognized this constantly repeating pattern, I could see how it showed up in all my relationships and in everything I did. After I gave this false vow the name Obligation, she moved into the front of my consciousness and turned into a pretty funny companion. I'd catch myself starting to say, "I *have to* clean the house,

SOUL VOWS

I *have to* get dinner on the table, I *have to* work on Saturday, I *have to* invite them for dinner . . . ," and I'd start laughing, Really? I *have* to put on a dinner party? I don't think so!

My mother's favorite word was *obey*, so I wasn't surprised when Obedience revealed herself to be a major false master. Kathleen in Texas was told repeatedly by relatives that she had to be the caretaker of the family mementos, keepsakes, and stories. In conversation with her false master Keeper, she realized this was why her life was filled with so much clutter. At last, she was ready to let go of all that stuff.

Here are some compassionate questions that may help you look beyond and beneath your stories to find the false vows you created in response to them:

> *Now that I see how my false beliefs began, help me see what they morphed into. What are the key repeating patterns in my life?*
>
> *How do I respond now, without even thinking, to stressful situations?*
>
> *What do I tell myself I have to do or say or ignore to feel safe?*
>
> *What false beliefs or habits have power in my life?*
>
> *When I look at the repeating patterns in my life, what does that tell me about my core false beliefs or vows?*
>
> *If each of my false beliefs had a name, what would it be?*

Visualize a little parade of false vows marching up from your womb in the second chakra, down your arm, and through your hand onto the page. Don't judge them as they show up. Just call them to the surface, greet them, and write them down. Some will be familiar old saws you picked up from your parents and teachers. Those might sound like "not good enough" or "money doesn't grow on trees" or "you have to fight for what you get in life." Others might be a surprise. You might find yourself blurting out, "Sheesh, I didn't even know that was in there!"

Or you might recognize an old familiar thorn and wonder why, after all the spiritual work you've done, that one is still there. When Dr. Marj Britt, creator of "Called By Love" was on

The Soul-Directed Life radio show, I asked her about these recurring shadows. She said this was completely normal and actually a good thing.

"As you go deeper and higher in the spiral path and experience more light, the light shines on more and more of the darkness," she said. "And what the light can touch can become integrated. So each time we see more light, that light shines on more shadow, and more and more integration occurs."

In *Breakthrough: Meister Eckhart's Creation Spirituality in New Translation,* Matthew Fox describes Meister Eckhart's path of spiritual journeying similarly: "It is *not* a journey up a ladder but a spiral of expanding consciousness that has no limits" (his italics). I find this spiral image very comforting. No matter how beautiful my spiritual life becomes, it can, and it will, always take me to new and deeper realms. There's always more heaven to be created on earth.

As your false unconscious vows march forward, write them all down. Don't let their appearance or name or persistent presence upset you. Don't judge them or argue with them or defend yourself. Don't waste time feeling shame or guilt. If you need an emotion to carry you through this adventure, try amazement. After all, it is astonishing how the human mind squeezes itself into all kinds of wacky shapes and hairpin curves to try to navigate through life. Be amazed at how creative you've been and have compassion for all the complex companions you've created.

How will you know you've captured all your false vows? You'll know. Your head critic will announce that the whole crew has arrived. If you have any doubts, ask it to go back and poke around inside and bring up the last few hiding in the crevices. Those may turn out to be your biggest and best teachers.

Notice How Your False Vows Drain Your Power and Keep You Fragmented

Once you have your false vows sitting around you in a circle, wearing their name tags, spend time with them. You will release and integrate them in a creative way in the third chakra, but don't rush to do that just yet. Instead, do the counterintuitive thing and sit with them. Observe them. Learn from them. Engage them in compassionate dialogue and ask them to show you how they have influenced the choices you've made. Ask them to point out how they created your perception of success and failure. Explore how they shifted the dynamics in all your relationships. Talk about how they keep showing up in your attitude, your confidence, and your sense of not being enough. Listen to how they impact what you believe is possible, how they draw your attention away from what you love and long for and drop it smack where you don't want it to be.

And pay attention to how you feel physically when you try to follow the directives of your false masters. Do you feel tired? In *Anatomy of the Spirit*, Caroline Myss explains, "What drains your spirit drains your body. What fuels your spirit fuels your body."

After several conversations with your false vows, how would you summarize their overall impact? I asked myself this question in my journal, but instead of answering it in words, I found myself drawing a cartoon outline of myself segmented into irregular disjointed pieces, like jigsaw puzzle pieces that didn't quite fit together. On each piece I wrote the name of one of my false masters: Obedience, Obligation, Neglect, Fear, Control, Living with Lies, Feeling Separate. Just looking at the drawing, I could see how my false vows kept me fragmented. I could see how hard it was just to move because I had to drag all these disconnected parts around with me. No wonder I was exhausted. No wonder I didn't feel centered or focused or whole. I wasn't!

Here are some soul writing suggestions that may help you find your own fragmented puzzle pieces:

Who are my primary false masters?

How does following my false vows impact me emotionally and physically?

If I could draw a picture of how I feel trying to follow the directives of all my false vows, what would it look like?

Ask for and Receive the Gifts of Your False Vows

Have you noticed that as you explore your false vows, you unearth not only all your long buried stories and patterns, but a few gifts as well? Is that a surprise?

It was for me. I wrote about my fears about money ad nauseam on the page, seeing Money Fear as a big bad bear in my life that I had to somehow conquer. But then one day I asked a different kind of question, "What did Money Fear teach me? What gifts did I receive from her?" Turns out Money Fear was practically a relative of Santa Claus for me. I quickly connected the dots between sitting up in bed, drenched in money sweats, to many of the attributes that make my beautiful writing life possible. What did worrying about money give me? An unquenchable thirst for knowledge, the ability to remain hyperfocused, the willingness to work incredibly hard, and the strength to put one foot in front of the other no matter what is happening. It also pushed me to take some astonishing risks that helped me see just how strong and capable I really am. My gift list gave me a whole new perspective on my so-called negative master and completely deflated any need to defeat her. Instead, I could bless her role in my life.

Meister Eckhart offers a beautiful symbol for this transition from battling our false masters to acknowledging their gifts. In a sermon titled "Sinking Eternally into God," he speaks of the Golden Rings of the lower powers. One lower power he mentions is anger. Anger is for many of us a very powerful and persistent false master. But instead of battling or rebuking or squashing the false master of Anger, Meister Eckhart suggests we put on a Golden Ring of Peace. Instead of succumbing to the false master of Greed, he suggests we put on a Golden Ring called Self-Content. Matthew Fox helps us understand Meister Eckhart's theology in his extensive commentaries for each sermon in *Breakthrough: Meister Eckhart's Creation Spirituality in New Translation.* On the Golden Ring concept, Matthew Fox says:

> One would think that Eckhart, like so many spiritual theologians, would fall into dualism when discussing the so-called "lower powers" of our psyches. But that is not the case. In fact, he invents a gentle image, an image of a reconciliation, namely that of a "golden ring" to describe how we are to live in harmony with these energies and not be putting them down in the name of ascetic practices.

I love this image. Instead of battling my false master of Money Fear, I can put on the Golden Ring of Confidence—a ring I might never have discovered if I hadn't wrestled so hard with Money Fear. Instead of battling with the false master of Obligation, I can acknowledge how her presence inspired me to explore the difference between *have to* and *want to* and put on a Golden Ring of Conscious Choice. As I move away from the false vow of Neglecting Myself, I can happily put on a Golden Ring called Self-Love. And as I loosen the grip of my first false master, Obedience, I put on a Golden Ring with the words *I Live My Truth* engraved inside. I am so grateful to Meister Eckhart and Matthew Fox for this sweet way to acknowledge the gifts of our false vows.

Alice in Illinois shared how her conversations with *Fraidy Kat* and her divine voice helped her uncover all her beautiful Golden Rings.

> Dear Kat,
> I'm working with the soul vows thing, and I really want to uncover my negative vows so I can move forward ... I want to be able to hear Spirit's guidance without you popping up with criticism and resistance.

A list of negative voices poured out on the page. As I was reading what was showing up, I remembered what Jesus taught: "agree with your adversaries quickly." I had perceived these negative voices as bitter enemies being angry with their messages and hating myself for allowing them to diminish my life.

So I wrote to the Voice: *I've come to unmask my enemies. I've been afraid of them for a long time. I've been hiding in the corner, waiting for them to go away, but they have not. I've decided to call them out one at a time to finally unmask them and make what has been ugly and painful something beautiful.*

So as I called them out to unmask their gifts I discovered:

From being silenced I found wisdom in listening,

From failure I found the power of imagination to provide rich ideas,

From fear I found the courage to overcome with faith.

From lack and limitation I found spiritual understanding.

From worry I found strength in the present moment.

From guilt I found unconditional love and forgiveness.

I wrote again to the Voice: *Now I know what agreeing with my adversaries means—it means making friends with what seems to cloud a beautiful, perfect life with fear, worry, and anxiety and understanding that their purpose is to help me see more clearly.*

Here is another evocative method of honoring the gifts of your false vows. It comes from Mirabai Starr in *God of Love*:

> Our gravest errors can leave scars that become our most beautiful gifts. And our scars become reminders of grace, of forgiveness. Our wounds can serve as signs of our interconnectedness with all beings, and motivate us to continue striving to make things right between us.

This is so aligned with John O'Donohue's reminder that our mistakes are our friends. In *Anam Cara*, he recommends that the sweet creative presence to bring to all your conversations with your false masters is compassion.

To help you hear and honor the gifts and rings and scars of your false vows, call each by name and tell it you understand that it was working to protect you in the best way it could. Then ask compassionate questions like these.

What benefits did I receive from you? What did you teach me?

How did you help me cope?

Is there something in these coping responses I can be grateful for?

How have you been my friend?

How did you try to protect me? Help me?

Did you leave a scar?

How can I acknowledge and bless my scars?

Do you have a Golden Ring for me? What is its name?

If I put on this Golden Ring, what will change?

When you finish, kiss each scar and put on the Golden Rings of your false vows.

Identify What You Want to Release and Make the Decision to Release

Would you like that cartoon of yourself as disjointed puzzle pieces to come together into a cohesive whole? That will happen in the third-chakra exploration. But before you move on, take a moment to summarize your adventures in this second-chakra exploration of creative choice.

You've had long, profound conversations with your critics and false masters. You've heard their stories, learned their names, tracked their presence in your life, received their gifts, and even kissed a few of their scars. You know them now almost as well as they know you. To complete this exploration, make a list of the false masters you want to transform and release in the third chakra. Are you ready to live a life free of their directives? Are you ready to take your attention away from your false masters and give it to your new and very beautiful soul-directed masters?

Are you ready to become what you love? These are big, big questions. Exploring them in deep soul writing will help you prepare for the beautiful experience of wholeness that awaits you.

> *I've been living with a lot of negative powers. Am I ready to say goodbye and really mean it? Am I ready to let go completely of these powers?*
>
> *My false masters have been the foundation of much of what I tell myself about myself. Who will I be without my stories?*
>
> *What do I think my life would look like, feel like, if these powers are no longer my primary drivers?*
>
> *Am I ready to release my false masters? How do I know I'm ready?*
>
> *I am ready to release my grip on the negative powers in my life. My journey with these false masters is complete:_____ (list them)*

Second Paradox: My Foe Is My Friend

This second-chakra exploration has been quite a dance with paradox, hasn't it? The more you danced with your critics and false masters, the more you discovered they have been your friends all along and even brought you important gifts. What began with judgment is ending with appreciation. What began with a feeling of trepidation is ending with gratitude. Your foe has revealed the friend inside. Just imagine what the world could look like if we all brought this "my foe is my friend" awareness into our public discourse. We could build a whole new and very beautiful world. And it is possible. I believe that. It is possible because *you* just planted a seed of it in your being. You brought a piece of heaven to earth.

Before you move on to the third chakra, stop for a moment and capture your dance with the paradox of the friend in the enemy, the light in the dark, the truth in the false, on this second-chakra triangle. For me, the second-chakra paradox sounds like "My foe is my friend" or "There's a friend in my foe." As I write those words, I hear again Thich Nhat Hanh's startling teaching, "To 'love our enemy' is impossible, because the moment we love him, he is no longer our enemy" (*Living Bud-*

dha, Living Christ). Isn't this exactly what happened? The "enemy" you have been dancing with has turned out to be yourself. Now you can take a deep breath and know that at last, you are no longer your own enemy.

The image I drew inside my triangle to illustrate my adventures in the second chakra is that cartoon outline of me as a jigsaw puzzle, but this time I drew the pieces fitting together. Please write your own paradox statements and draw your own picture to wrap up your dance with your false vows in this stunning chakra of choice.

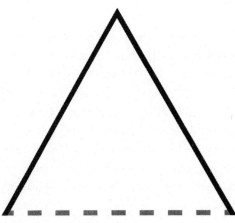

Second Discovery: I Am Free

As Alice completed her exploration of the second chakra, she found herself feeling a surprising sense of peace. She shared this beautiful entry from her journal:

> My soul is now free from anger and hate—I am whole.
> I have gathered the pieces of my self that have been at war,
> and now there is peace—sweet peace.

I recognized what she was describing. Once I made peace with my false masters, I could feel my pieces coming together into wholeness. Maybe it's not an accident that *piece* and *peace* are homonyms, like *altar* and *alter*. Peace does come when the pieces come together. I sense that this transformation is universal. It is a natural product of the paradoxical dance with an "enemy." The dance begins with frenetic movements, as you push and pull against your false master. But then, as you get to know your enemy, the dance slows and softens into a gentle sway, and you look at your enemy and realize you have a friend in your arms. In *God of Love*, Mirabai Starr describes this dénouement from fury and anger and hurt to peace: "Then one night you wake up and your heart is quiet. The worst thing that has happened to you is curled up, harmless, at your feet. You stroke it, open the door, and wave good-bye as it leaves."

Is this happening to you, too? Have the false vows that once held you in their relentless grip let go? Do they look pretty harmless now? Have they curled up at your feet? I don't think there is any great mystery or magic here. From the moment I knew my false vows' names, they could no longer hide out in my subconscious, directing things from their shadow bunkers. As John O'Donohue puts it, "When you can name your fear, your fear begins to shrink" (*Anam Cara*). Once I stopped fighting my false vows, looked into their eyes, and saw what I had created, I was free—free from their control and free to create something new.

Is that what you're discovering? Are you feeling free? Or at least free-er? Then say it. Say, "I am free." Say it again. It's an astonishing thing to hear yourself say. "I am free." Put that in your pocket along with "I am ready" and carry them into your exploration of the third chakra, the energy of your personal power.

Third Exploration

gather yourself into wholeness

Third Chakra: Solar Plexus Chakra
Third Paradox: Fragments are the sisters of wholeness.
Third Discovery: I am whole.

Because we have been dispersed, we need to be gathered. Because we have been fragmented, we need to become whole, to collect ourselves and thereby let our light be stronger.

Kabir Helminksi, *Living Presence*

In the first two explorations, you experienced how wrestling with the friction of paradoxical opposites generates a third different and deeply personal breakthrough insight. Now you've arrived at the third-chakra exploration, where the chakra *itself* is the product of the tension of the first and second.

The first chakra is often seen as connected with *earth*, because of its emphasis on lineage and grounding to mother earth. The second chakra is typically associated with *water*, because of all the fluid emotions and movement that happen there. The third is associated with *fire*, and that fire is generated by the interplay of the first and second chakras. Anoeda Judith explains this dynamic in *Wheels of Life*:

As we put together matter and movement, we find they create a third state: energy. If we rub two sticks together, we eventually get a spark that can ignite a fire. In the physical world, we call this combustion. In the body, it relates to metabolism. Psychologically it refers to the spark of enthusiasm that ignites power and will; in our behavior it is the realm of activity.

I would add that in the soul, this third-chakra energy is the fire of wholeness.

Fire transforms everything it touches. And whether we're conscious of it or not—and most of the time we're not—we use our personal will and third-chakra fire to transform our world. When we're conscious, we transform our surroundings into something that mirrors the beauty and will of our soul. When we're asleep, ruled by our false masters, we create something we don't like and don't want. In this third-chakra exploration, you'll learn to honor your fire power and begin to consciously use it to clear the way for your soul vows.

This transformative fire power is located in the solar plexus, just below the breastbone. You can see how essential this part of the body is to life. It is where the diaphragm supports the in-and-out life force of breath. It is the center of gravity in the body, the fulcrum point from which all forward motion comes. And it is your core. It's not an accident that yoga teachers, Pilates instructors, and personal trainers all tell us the key to a physically strong body is a strong core. The same is true on an energetic and spiritual level. The key to a meaningful and beautiful presence in this world is a strong spiritual core. In this chakra exploration you will develop a whole new understanding of what it means to live from your spiritual core.

The third chakra is also the energetic source behind how we show up in the world. As Carolyn Myss says in *Anatomy of the Spirit*, "[T]he third chakra relates to our personal power in relation to the external world." As we discovered in the second chakra, if we've been showing up in the world under the influence of several false masters, we've been showing up fragmented, disjointed, inconsistent, and erratic. When we are fragmented, we see the world as fragmented, and we jump from one piece to another to another as if we had SADD—spiritual attention deficit disorder.

Now that we know the names of our false masters and realize they are not and have never been our enemies, we can begin to show up in a whole new way—whole. When we are whole, we can see the world as whole, the cosmos as whole, the creator as whole, and we can begin to move through life with focus, clarity, and peace. That's the adventure ahead in the deep soul exploration of the third chakra: gathering all those fragmented pieces together and watching as the fire of transformation makes us whole.

Deep Soul Explorations

In this third deep soul exploration in the third chakra, you will:

- explore ways to transmute or release your false vows
- create a personal release ceremony
- prayerfully complete your relationship with your false vows
- relish feeling empty and whole

Explore Ways to Transmute or Release Your False Vows

In the last step in the second-chakra exploration, you made a decision to release your false masters. Now you are ready to say goodbye—and mean it. That full and final release takes place here in the chakra of transformation because releasing false masters is a major transformation, worthy of an investment of time to consider what you want to do and how you want to do it.

As you began to experience the freedom of no longer being under the unconscious domination of your false vows, did you start to imagine how you might complete the process and actually release them? There is no one right way. As with all things in a soul-directed life, the sweetest and best answer is the one you find when you go inside, ask your own big questions, and listen to the wisdom that bubbles up from your soul. That depth of exploration, coupled with the insights and wisdom of your master-teacher companion, will help you figure out how you want to honor and celebrate this major transformation.

I've been using the word *release* because I conducted a release ceremony for my seven false masters. I called it "Bury My Dead," and I'm going to share it with you. At the heart of the release ceremony was a powerful prayer, and as I spoke it aloud, I saw my old unconscious ways of living acknowledge their role was complete. I felt them quite literally step aside to create the empty space in which my beautiful soul vows could appear.

I loved that ceremony, but you might resonate more with the word *integrate* and want to create an integration ceremony, like the one Elizabeth Gilbert described in *Eat, Pray Love*. If you've read her book, the scene is probably burned in your memory. She sat alone on an isolated island in a self-imposed silent retreat and called forth every experience that had caused her sorrow. One by one, experiences of sadness, pain, anger, and shame came forward. As she acknowledged each one, she spoke to it kindly saying, "It's OK. I love you. I accept you. Come into my heart now. It's over." When she was finished, she felt empty. That's the clue that the transformation is complete: you feel *empty*. And it's another confirmation of the mysterious truth of Meister Eckhart's paradox: to be full you must be empty. When the experience was over, Gilbert said she looked into her heart and was surprised to see that even with all the sorrow and pain she had welcomed into it, there was still plenty of space. The heart's capacity to forgive and transmute is limitless. This, she realized, is how the Divine loves—without limit. Your love-filled soul vows will soon flow through your own limitless heart. But first, you must become empty.

How would you like to release your false vows? Integrate them? Transform them? Befriend them? Marielle in New

Brunswick, Canada, decided to welcome all her false masters into her heart. She sat with her "beasts" for quite a while, spoke to them with love, and watched as they simply melted away in the presence of her tenderness and love. She was surprised to see them "transformed into beauty." At the end of her befriending ceremony, Marielle said, "I do feel free, and there is new clean space for my soul vows. I feel whole at the same time because I didn't give up a part of me. I appreciated my beasts for their gifts and loved them as the beasts they are, and I think only then did they transform into love."

Eiman in Abu Dhabi sent formal written invitations to each of her false masters, inviting them to a "Come to the Light" ceremony.

Gail in Massachusetts created a multifaceted ceremony in which she released some false vows and transformed or even adopted others, according to the purpose and value of each false vow in her life.

Here are a few soul writing questions to help you explore the possibilities and hear your soul's preferences:

Am I ready to be empty of my false vows in order to be full of my soul vows?

What is the nature of my false masters?

How would they like to be recognized, acknowledged, and transformed?

What type of process would complete our relationship and free them of any compunction to continue to manage my life?

Do my false masters want to be transmuted, released, or something else?

What kind of ceremony would help me gather my fragments into wholeness?

What kind of ceremony would leave me feeling empty and ready to be filled with my beautiful new soul vows?

Create a Personal Release Ceremony

Now that you know the nature of your false vows and how they want to complete a lifelong relationship with you, you are ready to create a holy ritual to honor their presence and gifts and lovingly release them to their own spiritual evolution. Maybe they return to the Divine. Maybe they dissolve like sugar in water. Maybe they find a soft place in your heart where they can be loved, but no longer needed to manage things.

This is a creative, delightful time in your soul vows experience. Later, you will have the opportunities to create two more rituals: your soul vows declaration ceremony and your daily soul vows practice. I do hope you love and embrace ritual. It is an essential part of the spiritual life. All spiritual traditions have ceremonial rituals. Some are elaborate, some elegant and simple. Perhaps your own tradition will influence how you create your false vows ceremony. Or you may prefer to create something fresh and unique, something you design just for this sacred experience. Here are a few ways members of my Soul Vows courses have completed their journey with their false vows. Perhaps they will spark your own creative fire.

Lily wanted to hold her release ceremony at a location that would have great significance for her. She drove to Walden Pond State Reservation, not far from her home in Massachusetts, at 3:00 A.M., when the park was closed. She said "entering the park after hours was a symbolic breaking of all those old vows." She began by reading this quote from Ralph Waldo Emerson:

> Do not be too timid and squeamish about your actions. All life is an experiment. The more experiments you make the better. What if they are a little coarse, and you may get your coat soiled or torn, What if you do fail, and get fairly rolled in the dirt once or twice? Up again, you shall never be so afraid of a tumble.

Then she read Coleman Barks' translation of Rumi's "The Guest House," from *The Essential Rumi,* out loud:

> This being human is a guest house.
> Every morning a new arrival.

A joy, a depression, a meanness,
some momentary awareness comes
as an unexpected visitor.

Welcome and entertain them all!
Even if they are a crowd of sorrows,
who violently sweep your house
empty of its furniture,
still, treat each guest honorably.
He may be clearing you out
for some new delight.

The dark thought, the shame, the malice.
meet them at the door laughing and invite them in.

Be grateful for whatever comes.
because each has been sent
as a guide from beyond.

Then Lily began speaking her own opening prayer. This is the first paragraph:

The night has come to bury my dead, to honor these beloved and not-so-beloved friends who have visited often and proffered on the house gifts of astounding scents and colors, who have loved me the best they knew how, who have indeed served me well. But their services are obsolete and no longer required. Their spirits are welcome to visit now and again, servants on the path of awakening, but their vitality which once consumed me is gone, I am no longer bound by them, their corpses stinking reminders of the promises they once held.

With her opening prayer complete, she called forward each of her false vows: Fear, Powerlessness, Resentment, Distrust, Scarcity, Anxiety, Obligation, Shame. She addressed each by name, spoke of its role in her life—both the gifts and the blockages—

and ended asking Tankashelah, the Great Mystery, to absorb the false one. Here is one example:

Oh, Distrust, dear Distrust,

You have protected me from fanaticism, false and harmful beliefs,

and you have taught me to be fluid,

attaching not to one idea, but basking in the wonders of many.

You have taught me the gift of discernment:

Who to spend my time with. How to spend my time.

When you distrust, these questions become very important.

But you have kept me from being present.

You have kept me from my heart.

It is time to stop anticipating negative outcomes

and to *trust life,* to know the universe is a good and friendly place.

I breathe life fully in this moment.

Tankashelah, hear my prayers.

When she had spoken to all her false vows, Lily lit a piece of paper with their eight names and scattered the ashes to the four directions. Knowing she was ready to hear her soul vows, she declared herself empty and ready with this invocation: "May my true soul vows emerge from behind these clouds and may the now-forming rainbow remind me who I truly am."

Lily concluded her ceremony by stepping into the pond to baptize herself. Suddenly she heard what sounded like an angry man's deep voice. She froze. It was a goose greeting the sunrise. When Lily got back home she looked up goose medicine in Ted Andrew's *Animal Speak*: "A goose as a totem can reflect that you are about to break free of old childhood restraints and come into your own. Anytime the goose comes in as a totem, you can expect to have the imagination stirred towards new travels to distant places—whether in body or mind." The goose turned out to be quite prophetic; Lily traveled to three countries that year.

A woman in upstate New York wrote all she wanted to release on small squares of paper. The next day she went for a long walk in her favorite woods. As she walked, she spoke to her false vows with tenderness, reviewing their long history and reminding the vows of all they had done for her. When she came upon a fallen tree that was slowly being returned to mother earth, she slipped a square under it so it too could become earth. Other squares she pushed down among tree roots. The last square she pushed under an insect nest. When all her false vows were safely resting in their new homes, she said a prayer of thanksgiving and returned home. That night she had a lovely dream. She felt her false vows were honoring this new separation and somehow blessing her and saying goodbye.

A gardener carved the names of her false vows into vegetables and then shredded them for compost to physically honor how her false vows had given her many rich nutrients to nourish the soil of her life. When her new vegetables began to sprout the next season, she laughed joyously at the holy transformation that had occurred in mother earth without her seeing or doing or managing anything.

Paula in Florida wrote a short play and asked the women in her therapy group to hold a sign and speak the lines of each of her false vows. As each false vow spoke, Paula tied a string around the actor's wrist and tied the other end to her own waist. When all the false vows had spoken, Paula asked the actors to turn around. Then she cut all the strings and asked the actors to take the strings off their hands and toss them to the ground. When they turned around, Paula was wearing a giant gold bow on her head to represent all the gifts she had been given by her false vows and the gift she felt her whole self could now be to the world.

When it was time to release her false masters, Marleen was at John of God's center in Brazil with a group from her Denver church. She sent this email from Brazil:

The old vows were pretty intense, and I was having a hard time releasing them. I could physically feel the pain of the old stuff—the feeling of not being good enough, hiding, overly sensitive to criticism, and self-judgment. I decided to release them at the sacred waterfall in Abadiania. I put my head under the waterfall and released fear and all its forms of fear. The second time I put my head under the waterfall, I brought in love and all its forms. That was my entire ceremony. And it felt holy and complete and good.

If I were creating my release ceremony today, I might not call it "Bury My Dead." I now have a gentler, more unitive view of my false vows. I no longer see them as something to bury; I see them as parts of me to own, embrace, and comfort. But every time I read the prayer-poem from my ceremony in my Soul Vows courses, I am overwhelmed by the reaction. Somehow this poem hands people the freedom to create their own release ceremony. Perhaps that is because each release, as Kabir Helminski reminds us in *Living Presence*, is a little death: "We must first recognize, respect, and surrender these negative states. We release them by recognizing them, and each surrender is a little death."

In my release prayer, I asked my seven-year-old self to join me as we look at all our dead fears and see that they're not so scary after all. In fact, they're rather pathetic. In the end, they had no power, while we survived. Writing this prayer gave me many gifts. It gave me the huge gift of freedom from my false masters, but I think it gave me something even more valuable. It opened my heart to a deep compassion for my little self who grew up in a house filled with fear. My father, like so many of his generation, thought he had to be the head of the household, the enforcer, and the only breadwinner. Everything and everyone had to be under his control. To bear this unbearable load, he reinforced himself with alcohol and prescriptions. When he felt control slipping out of his fingers, he responded with rage and sometimes violence. The only safe way to live in this house was to be quiet, invisible, compliant, and very, very obedient. No wonder my child-self created these false masters. In this prayer, she and I get to say goodbye to them. The being who was welcomed into my heart after being ostracized and isolated for so many years wasn't any false master; it was my newly free, suddenly empty, and surprisingly whole child-adult self. (You can hear me read this prayer at janetconner.com.)

Bury My Dead: A Prayer of Endings

Dear God, I've come to bury my dead.

They lived with me a long time. They tried to serve me well.

I am not angry with them. Not anymore. I was at first.

Angry that I had given them such power. Angry that I had let them move in.

But look at the sweet girl who obliged them. Who can be angry with her?

Not me. I can only hug her and bless her and tell her all is finally well.

Let's go in the house together, child.

What do we see?

Dead and decaying corpses everywhere.

Place smells bad, looks bad, feels awful.

It is time to cart the dead away.

Let's pick them up, child, and bury them.

In the basement is the wretched body of Obedience.

He used to be such a commanding presence.

"Obey!" he would scream, and obey I did.

Now he doesn't look so scary.

Rather pathetic, actually, with bulging eyes, decaying mouth, exploded tongue.

He commands nothing and no one now.

Let's bury him, child.

Goodbye, Obedience, goodbye.

In the kitchen lies the skeleton of Obligation.

Look at her, child, how she struggled to hold things together.

She had to work, cook, clean, had to finish one more thing and start another.

Isn't it lovely to see her finally stop, slump in a chair, and refuse to go on?

She doesn't have to do anything anymore.

Let's bury her, child.

Goodbye, Obligation, goodbye.

Look in the doorway, crumpled on the floor: that's what's left of Neglect.

She was so focused on the outside, taking care of everyone and everything,

that finally there was no inside, no strength, no core.

She couldn't hold on, couldn't continue.

Looks like she's disintegrated to nothing.

Let's bury this dust, child.

Good bye, Neglect, goodbye.

Let's go in the bedroom, child, and find the frightened one.

Poor thing, look at her quivering bones.

She lived in Fear: fear of stopping, fear of changing, fear of the known,

fear of the unknown. Afraid to stay. Afraid to go.

Now, at last, she is still. Fear no longer fills her veins.

Let's bury her, child.

Goodbye, Fear, goodbye.

Oh look, child, fallen in the hallway: it's Control.

She's completely out of control now.

No longer looking perfect. No longer trying to manage everyone and everything.

Things have finally spiraled completely out of control.

Unable to make anything happen, she collapsed where she stood.

Let's surrender her to the earth, child, where she can rest.

Goodbye, Control, goodbye.

Oh dear, look who's on the phone—was on the phone—the Lying one.

Her lies smell so terrible; we may not be able to get near.

Her words have rotted her tongue.

Her teeth collapsed around the hole in her truth.

Let's bury her quickly in the warm soil.

Goodbye, Lies, goodbye.

Let's go up to the attic, child. There is one last dead thing: the Separated one.

See, she wrapped herself in blankets, stuffed her sobs with cloth.

She thought she was completely separated, completely alone.

But the light was all around, is all around. See?

The light is shining through the windows, sparkling through the cracks.

Why couldn't she see it? Why did she suffer so?

Let's bury her now, child.

Goodbye, Separation, goodbye.

Dear God, the child and I have come to bury my dead.

We surrender them to the care of your healing earth.

Dust they were and dust they shall become.

They tried to serve me.

In pain and effort they captured my attention.

In pain and effort they taught me, finally taught me, to say NO.

And I do say NO.

No to Obedience.

No to Obligation.

No to Neglecting myself.

No to Fear.

No to Control.

No to Lies.

No to the Belief that I was Alone.

None of these ideas were true.

None of these things were real.

None of these monsters were alive.

I made them true.

I made them real.

I gave them life.

Every time I was afraid, I gave them life.

I am not afraid any more.

I call my power back to me.

Away from Obedience.

gather yourself into wholeness   89

Away from Obligation.

Away from Neglect.

Away from Fear.

Away from Control.

Away from Lies.

Away from Believing I am Alone.

I am not alone.

You are with me always, dear God, giving me strength to bury my dead.

During my release ceremony, as I spoke to my child self about each of our "dead," I wrote the name of that false master on a piece of paper and burned them one by one in a copper bowl in my backyard. I didn't want the ashes in my ground, so I put them a new white envelope and prayerfully placed the envelope in the garbage.

What kind of ceremony would honor the completion of your old relationship with your false masters? You are your own priest-priestess-shaman, so step into your divine power and design your own release-transmutation-integration ceremony. This third chakra is about gathering yourself back to wholeness, so perhaps you'd like to create a "Return to Wholeness" or "Gathering Myself Back to Wholeness" or just "Wholeness" ceremony. This is a lovely topic to talk over with your voice on the page. You might also ask for guidance in a dream and lie still on the pillow in the morning, allowing the images to return to you. Or you might listen in the shower or in the car or while walking or simply sitting outside. Once your heart is open, all you have to do is pay attention.

Here are a few deep soul writing questions that may help you create a beautiful ceremony that leads you gently back to who you really are and who you always have been—your whole and holy self.

What is my intention in this ceremony?

Am I releasing, transmuting, integrating—or some combination of intentions?

How will my ceremony move me toward wholeness?

How will this ceremony move me toward becoming empty?

What expectations do I have for this ceremony?

What do I think it means to be "whole" or "empty"?

What actions do I want to take in my ceremony?

Do I need any props?

Where do I want to hold my ceremony?

When do I want to hold my ceremony? Does the date or time hold any symbolism?

Do I want to be alone or have witnesses? Who would understand and honor what I am doing? (Don't take this question lightly. Do not invite people, not even your partner, just because you think you should. Only invite soul friends who will love and support you through this ceremony and honor your intention. If you have the slightest doubt, do your ceremony alone.)

What prayers or invocations do I want to say?

Do I want to read from any sacred texts?

What does my master-teacher companion have to contribute to this ceremony?

Do I want music, songs, hymns, chants?

Will there be dancing or movement?

Do I want poetry or other readings?

Will I be drawing or painting or making anything?

Will I be inviting my false masters to speak?

Do I want to end with a closing prayer or celebration?

Is there a memento of this ceremony I'd like to keep on my altar?

What shall I name my ceremony? What words capture its purpose or essence?

Prayerfully Complete Your Relationship with Your False Vows

Once you've designed your ceremony, you have the joyous opportunity to bring it to life. I have just one word of caution to whisper in your ear as you step into your blessed event: release all your expectations about what it should look like or what should happen. I can promise you that whatever you think will or should happen won't—not exactly anyway. And that is a good thing. This is a soul ceremony. Even if you bring a script, a carefully chosen pile of books, and a basket of props, things will not go as planned. Oh, they might follow your outline, and on the surface, you might think things are going as planned. But the place where the real action is happening isn't the ground you're standing on; the real changes are taking place in your soul and your heart. And on that sacred ground, you are not in charge.

Here are a few ideas that may help you create the sacred space for your holy release ritual. Select any that feel right to you.

- Begin by setting your *intention* for the highest good for you and your soul's journey, and for the false masters who have completed their relationship with you and are now ready for the next step in their own evolution.

- Call in your *angels and guides* to be with you, support you, and hold you close throughout the ceremony.

- Create *sacred space* by blessing your physical space. You can do that with sound, such as singing, ringing bells, or tapping crystal bowls. You can also bless your space with holy waters and sacred oils or candles and crystals. If you have some ceremonial herbs like dried sage or sweetgrass to burn, that might be a lovely way to begin. And perhaps you'd like to mark the physical space with prayer flags or a sacred shape or word you draw on the ground or a symbol you tie to a stick and place in the spot.

- Do an oracle *card reading* from a treasured deck or read from a *sacred text* to welcome divine guidance into the ceremony. The reading may well trigger a new understanding of what your ceremony is really all about.

- Slowly and prayerfully read a significant passage from your soul vows master-teacher companion or other book or mystical poetry. Mark the page you read. It will be a treasure forever.

- When you are ready, enter into the *release* portion of your ceremony. Speak words of release or integration or transmutation and conduct your ceremonial actions. Take your time. Don't rush. Give yourself time to enter into this experience, honoring its profundity, and allowing something real to happen inside you.

- As you go through your ceremony, *notice yourself.* How is your body reacting? Is your breath changing? Are your muscles relaxing? Are you thirsty? Be sure to drink plenty of water before, during, and after your ceremony. How do you feel? Are tears rising? Do you feel more open, lighter, more peaceful? Do you feel the fire of transmutation in your third chakra? Do you feel like laughing or singing or dancing for joy?

- If you have *witnesses,* honor their presence and ask them to contribute to the ritual. Perhaps they could sign a special book or card. Perhaps they could take turns reading sacred poetry or speaking a personal blessing they've written for you to mark this moment. Or perhaps they could pass a special stone and imbue it with sacred prayers for you.

- After the ceremony, don't rush back into ordinary life. Give yourself plenty of quiet and solitude to *contemplate* the transformative power of releasing your old false masters. A long contemplative walk in nature or by the sea might be restorative. Or just sit still in a chair and stare out the window or at a holy image.

- To capture the full wisdom of release, have a long *deep soul writing* conversation filled with gratitude and joy. Talk about how it feels to be free, empty, and whole.

- *Celebrate.* You have done something of great importance to your soul. Honor it with a special meal or celebratory toast or dance—something playful and fun.

- *Sleep.* Initially release can feel energizing; but you may find you need more sleep for a few days as your body adjusts to the cellular and soul-ular changes that happened during the ceremony. Give yourself all the silence and rest you need.

After the ceremony ends, find ways to honor the experience and keep it alive in your heart. Write yourself a special letter. Speak about the experience and what it means and how you now feel. Tell yourself why you did this, what you released or transmuted, and why it matters. Give yourself sweet messages of congratulations, support, and love. Then tuck the letter away and open it a year from now on the anniversary of your wholeness ceremony.

In the days and weeks after your ceremony, notice the aftereffects. Don't be surprised if your body does some releasing of its own. After all, those old masters were taking up cellular as well as soul-ular space. This is an excellent time to eat mindfully, drink lots of water, move your body, and get more sleep. After sweeping away decades of old programming is it easier to hear and trust your guidance? Do you hear your soul speaking more clearly? Keep a record of not only the changes in you and in how you react to the world, but also in how the world reacts to you. The day will come when you will want to remember this experience, so record it now, while the experiences are fresh.

Relish Feeling Empty and Whole

What happens *after* you release your false masters? The first thing members of Soul Vows courses say is they feel less scattered, more present, more aware of themselves and of the world around them. This heighted awareness is not hypervigilant; it's gentle. You stop scanning your surroundings for things to be afraid of or defend against or hold at bay. Instead, you are able to stand still and really see what is happing in all its complexity, without your old automatic reactions jumping in to take charge. This doesn't mean pretending there is no suffering or pain. Quite the opposite. Freed from all your old internal noise, you may find you actually notice more pain in the world, but instead of trying to protect yourself from it, compassion and kindness well up inside and move you to help.

People also say they feel lighter—lighter in their bodies, lighter in their hearts, lighter in their minds. They report that waves of worry or anger rarely come over them, and when fear and fury do visit, they are able to see what's happening and bring themselves back to center more quickly and easily than before.

They also report an interesting dichotomy. Although they feel more patient with the external world, they feel a more intense internal desire for a deeper, more meaningful relationship with the Divine. They have become impatient for God. Kabir Helminksi describes this transformation in *Living Presence*:

> Freed of our habitual thoughts, expectations, opinions, constructions, and fears, consciousness is freed to receive deeper impressions. New meanings begin to flow into consciousness from the unconscious. Extrasensory experience may be heightened. Whether we are aware of it or not, we become more sensitive to others' thoughts and emotions. We may be able to respond to others more sensitively and wisely, because we are less dominated by our old habitual patterns of thought and feeling. At this stage we are flooded with rich meanings, and life can take on a new depth.
>
> There really is no end to the refinement that is possible. One more and more begins to perceive qualitatively the ultimate reality, which we are preparing to apprehend and which is all that is, has certain qualities such as peace, compassion, creativity, vitality, generosity, glory, subtlety, wisdom, beauty, and unity.
>
> Through this deeper refinement of attention and an ever more subtle focusing, the false identity collapses. The supports on which it once depended have been removed, and the self begins to feel like a unique point of view of the Whole, a reflector of cosmic awareness.

That's where we're going next: into the state of reflecting the Whole, the Divine, the cosmic awareness. That's what "living your soul vows" means. But for now, bask in the precious feeling of being a whole and empty vessel in which this divine reflection can appear. You have gathered your fragmented self together. You have honored the disconnected pieces you once labeled negative.

Here are a few soul writing questions to help you capture what it feels like to be whole:

> *How do I feel right now?*
>
> *Do I feel lighter?*
>
> *Am I more aware of myself and others?*
>
> *Do I feel more connected when I pray or soul write?*
>
> *Am I less anxious, less vigilant, less judgmental?*
>
> *Do I feel empty? Gathered? Whole?*
>
> *What does it mean to be empty, gathered, and whole?*

Third Paradox: Fragments Are the Sisters of Wholeness

When you danced with your "enemy" in the second paradox, did you notice how you were gently guided onto a bigger dance floor, a cosmic dance floor—the floor of wholeness? As you danced, your partner transformed from ogre to friend, the music shifted from frantic to smooth, and the floor itself expanded and became more beautiful. And in the most wondrous change of all, as you began to trust the dance, you began to melt into your partner. It's been a glorious glide, hasn't it? But just think, this sweet feeling of your whole self happened because you were willing to see and bless your fragmented self. Your whole self is a close sister or brother to your piecemeal self.

I stumbled upon this understanding of two opposites as "sisters" while I was waiting for my son to be released from prison. When the federal judge sent Jerry to prison on May 21, 2013, to coerce him to talk about his political activist friends, I desperately needed comfort. One author I can count on to soothe my soul is John O'Donohue, so I turned to *Eternal Echoes*. In a chapter on "A Philosophy of Loss," I stumbled upon this sentence: "Loss is the sister of discovery."

I stopped reading and stared out the window. Here was the key to understanding waiting. I whispered, "Waiting is the sister of . . . ?" And then I knew: "waiting is the sister of welcoming." Thanks to John O'Donohue, I stopped wanting waiting to go away. Instead, I invited her in—all the way in. I had conversations with waiting. I got to know her at depth and I let her see me at depth. Waiting became my friend. She patted my back on the hard days and held me upright each morning as I said the Perfect Prayer for my Jerry. She held my hand every day and reminded me that we would have much to welcome.

Jerry's legal team worked for months on a rare motion outlining all the losses he had borne in prison without wavering on his commitment to silence. Clearly he could not be coerced to speak; therefore, leaving him in prison was punishing him— something the judge did not have the authority to do. The motion was submitted on December 20, 2013. We heard nothing for a month, and I was ready to give up. But then, on Tuesday, January 28, 2014, a federal marshal escorted Jerry from his cell to the lobby of the courthouse, unlocked his handcuffs, and said, "You're free." The judge had released Jerry. And I got to dance with the sweet sister of waiting—welcoming. And you are now dancing with wholeness because you were willing to dance with her sister, fragments.

How will you capture this wild and wonderful transformative fire of your third-chakra exploration? On my triangle, I wrote "I am my fragments" on one side and "I am whole" on the other. And then across the bottom, on the line that captures the new arising out of the dance of these opposites, I wrote "My fragments are the sisters of my wholeness." In the middle, I drew that cartoon outline of myself from the second chakra, only this version has no dotted lines. Thanks to the dance with my fragments, I gathered myself and I am both empty and whole.

What statements describe the paradox of fragments begetting wholeness in this third chakra for you? And what image captures the wonderful dance from scattered and fragmented to empty and whole?

My fragments are the sisters
of my wholeness

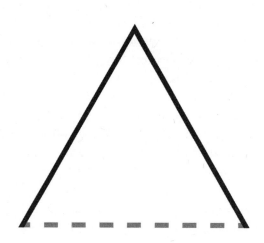

soul vows

Third Discovery: I Am Whole

In the first chakra you put "I am ready" in your pocket. In the second, you added "I am free." If the first and second chakras are the spark that creates the fire of the third chakra, then rubbing your first two discoveries together should create the spark of the third discovery. And it does. Because you were *ready* to embrace your divine lineage, and you were willing to be *free* of your false masters, you transformed yourself into an empty *whole* container. Your attention is whole. Your mind is whole. Your heart is whole. Even your body is whole.

Does it feel good and powerful to be whole? Does it feel warm and exciting to be empty, ready to let your heart be filled with your beautiful soul vows? Then say it. Say, "I am whole." Say, "I am empty." Say, "I am a whole and empty vessel for the Presence of the Divine." Say it in your own words, but say it.

Meister Eckhart wraps up our adventures in the third chakra with this simple truth: "Wholeness is holiness." Look at that! You've danced your way to whole and holy! Put "I am whole" in your pocket and carry it into the fourth-chakra exploration, where your soul vows are waiting in your whole and holy heart.

Fourth Exploration

listen from your heart

Fourth Chakra: Heart Chakra
Fourth Paradox: 1 + 1 = 1
Fourth Discovery: I am open.

*The heart is the center of our being and our most comprehensive
cognitive faculty. The eye of the heart sees more truly than
our ego-based intellect and emotions. With such a heart, true
surrender, and true happiness and well-being, become possible.*

Kabir Helminksi, *The Knowing Heart*

In the fire of the third chakra you burned away the false beliefs
holding you back, and in the process you forged your very being
into an empty vessel ready to receive the divine gift of your soul
vows. This gift will arrive here in the fourth chakra, the chakra
of the heart.

This is a most interesting chakra. It is the chakra at the center
of your spiritual being, with three energy fields below and three
above. Yoga teachers often describe the three lower chakras as
linking us to our humanity and gathering the energy flowing up
from mother earth, while the three higher chakras connect us to
our divinity and receive the energy flowing down from the heavens and gathering them together in the heart. That dual energy

101

flow is illustrated in the ancient Hindu symbol of the fourth chakra: two overlapping triangles. Harish Johari explains the symbolism of the two triangles in *Chakras*: "One points upward symbolizing Shiva, the male principle. The other triangle points downward and symbolizes Shakti, the female principle. The star represents the balance that is attained when these two principles are joined in harmony." In *Wheels of Life*, Anodea Judith puts it this way: "The triangles represent the descent of spirit into the body and the ascent of matter rising to meet spirit."

Today we often call the overlapping triangles symbol the Star of David, but in its pre-Judaic origins, it symbolized the sacred marriage of the divine feminine and divine masculine. In her discussion of the fourth chakra in *Anatomy of the Spirit*, Caroline Myss expands our understanding of this ancient archetype of the sacred marriage into a modern archetype of true partnership that begins with the partnership with the self: "The symbolic meaning of the sacrament of Marriage is that one must be in union with one's own personality and spirit first."

This is a perfect description of what happens in the fourth chakra and throughout the rest of your soul vows adventure. At the center of your spiritual heart, you know—and you know that you know—that you are the beloved of the Divine. This is the great romance—the *first* romance—the romance of soul and Spirit, lover and Beloved. In this great romance your soul vows are your very own sacred, mystical marriage vows, heard and felt in your sacred, mystical heart.

To locate the presence of the fourth chakra, put your arms out spread-eagle, like the Leonardo da Vinci's famous "Vitruvian Man." That figure is said to illustrate Leonard's profound understanding of proportion. If we humans are perfectly proportioned, might that not be another sign of our dual human-divine lineage? Look at yourself in a full-length mirror with your arms outstretched. (If your body can't hold that position, simply look into the mirror and see yourself as Leonardo's beautiful form.) Your arms form a perfect horizontal line; your feet and head a clear vertical line. And where do they meet? In your heart.

Now imagine a flow of earth energy rising through your feet and a simultaneous flow of celestial energy descending through your head. Watch as the two flows meet in the only place they can—your holy heart. This explains why your heart is so wise. It knows. It knows effortlessly. And it knows multitudes more than your brain. Scientists at the Institute of Heartmath discovered that the heart generates an electromagnetic field thousands of times stronger than the field of the brain. Your heart is a finely tuned organ of spiritual intelligence and discernment, and this fourth-chakra soul vows exploration is the perfect time to learn how to really use it.

In this exploration you will listen with the ears of your radiant heart to the song of your soul vows. It may sound faint at the moment, just a slight hum in the distance, but by the time you leave this chakra you will be singing your own "Ode to Joy" with gusto. Only the lyrics won't be a poem immortalized by Beethoven; they will be the lyrics of your very own soul vows heard for the first time in the chambers of your holy heart.

Deep Soul Explorations

In this fourth deep soul exploration in the fourth chakra, you will:

- invite a wide range of values and ways of being to step forward
- get to know each potential soul vow
- sort and sift your big pot of values into a focused list
- embrace Spirit's living presence in your soul vows
- write your soul vows

Invite a Wide Range of Values and Ways of Being to Step Forward

When you released the false vows that kept you fragmented, you became a lovely, gathered, open, and receptive space ready to be filled with your soul's most precious and important values. In this sweet state of emptiness, you can be still and hear the desires of your soul.

And your soul has plenty to say. It wants to commit to values. It wants to walk this earth in integrity and harmony. It wants to be the highest and most authentic you it can be. How do you know that? Oh, you know. You know exactly what it feels like when you make choices that are not in sync with your authentic self. Your heart literally hurts. So if you know what being out of sync feels like, it follows that your heart will recognize your beautiful in-sync values immediately.

Where to begin? The possibilities are endless, aren't they? There are so many lovely values: to be kind, generous, honest, grateful, joyful, to search for truth, to pray, to trust, to heal, to surrender, to forgive, to partner, to share, to serve, to embrace the mystery, to love unconditionally, to be open, to be receptive, to be willing, to be worthy. You could easily come up with fifty beautiful ways of being. But if you tried to commit to fifty or even twenty soul vows every day, you would quickly become overwhelmed and unfocused. In this fourth-chakra exploration, you will begin with a nice long list, but gradually the list will sort and sift itself into a short list that sets your heart on fire.

There is no one right path to your soul vows. They are, after all, *your* soul's deepest knowing. They spring from your soul's desire to commit to live in a way that is congruent with its deepest truths. If anything I offer in this chapter helps you hear those truths, take it. But if something seems to get in the way, please pass it by. Learning to honor the call to pass by is, in itself, good practice for recognizing your soul vows. In the coming days you will call forward dozens of lovely possibilities, but if you are not *in love* with them, if your heart does not soar in recognition, then you will gently let them pass by, sending them on their way to find the soul for whom they are intended.

Begin by Creating Sacred Space

Enter your cave of solitude and pray for guidance and grace. State your intention for this next step in your soul's romance.

Announce that you are open and ready to hear the sweet song of your soul vows. And then begin. But remember, you are no longer speaking to any false masters or unconscious pushes and pulls. You are now speaking to your whole and holy Self. For many, a delightful flow of values is sparked by an open, warm invitation, such as this soul-writing suggestion:

> Beloved Soul Vows,
> I know that you are waiting for me to notice you, hear you, recognize and embrace you. I am here. I am here for you. I am here for my royal, divine soul and for my deepest knowing. Speak to me. I am listening. What do I need to know right now about my soul's most precious values?

As you write, listen to the responses with an open heart. Welcome whatever comes. Your task is not to try to find the "right" values or the "most holy" ones. Nor is it your job to carefully edit so that only qualities of the "highest" vibration remain. If you edit possibilities as they arise, you will inadvertently set aside a jewel waiting to come to life through you. Kabir Helminski, in *The Knowing Heart,* helps us remember the true source of our soul vows:

> It is important to consider that we do not originate or create these qualities; we reflect them. . . . We can only discover them as they are revealed to us; then we can reflect them in this existence. From one perspective all these qualities exist in the invisible, transpersonal treasury of Being. It is we who bring them into existence and manifestation by removing the obstacles presented by the false self.

Here are a few more soul-writing suggestions that may help you hear and gather the jewels bubbling up from what Helminksi calls the "treasury of Being" and onto your journal pages:

> What are my core truths?

What are the deepest most beautiful values of my soul?

What is an authentic life?

What would I be doing if my life were a full reflection of who I really am?

What would my life look like if I walked hand-in-hand with the Divine all day long?

What values want to walk this life with me? Why these?

Start Filling Your Big Pot

As anything comes to the surface that could potentially be a soul vow, record it in your journal. Set aside five pages or more for this purpose. Label these pages "My Big Pot of Soul Vows." Or you might get a real pot or bowl or basket and fill it with strips of paper as ideas come your way. Don't weigh or edit anything yet. If a phrase or sentence or word arrives on the page, or leaps at you from a billboard, or pops into your mind, or pokes you in a dream, toss it in your big pot. Sifting and winnowing will come later. For now, just gather.

Study the Contrast Between What You Released and Its Opposite

If jumping into a conversation about your soul vows seems a bit overwhelming, consider starting with a more narrow focus: what you *don't* want. You know what that is; you just released it. You know you don't want your unconscious masters in your life any more, so perhaps their opposites can tell you something about how your divine Self *does* want to live.

Draw two columns in your journal and label them "Dead" and "Living." Write your false masters on the "Dead" side and then quickly, without judgment or evaluation, jot down the opposite—the positive value your divine Self would naturally exhibit—under "Living." You may or may not end up using any of these in your final soul vows, but many people find this contrast exercise helps them kick start a flow of ideas.

Afterward, review your table of contrasts. Are there any surprises? Anything grab you or shout "notice me"? Do you see any recurring themes?

In my case, several of my dead false masters—Obligation, Obedience, Neglect, Lying, and Control—called forward two soul vows: "I live in partnership," because partners don't act that way, and "I honor myself," because if I truly honor myself, I can't neglect myself or allow others to control me or feel obligated to satisfy other people's desires.

Look at your table of contrasts as a gestalt, a whole, and see if your old, negative masters are helping you see an essential way of being or two that is nonnegotiable, that simply *must* be how you live. Have a conversation on the page about the deeper meaning of your contrast table. There just might be a vein of gold—a Golden Ring or two—running through your old false masters that pops up here and asks you to consider it for your soul vows.

Here are a few questions that may help you find the gold in your contrast table:

How did I feel making this table?

Are there any surprises?

Do I see a pattern, a recurring theme?

If I don't want to live directed by my false vows anymore, how do I want to live?

What are my false vows trying to tell me through this exercise?

Are any potential soul vows winking at me through this table?

Turn to Your Master-Teacher Companion

Another source for your big pot of possibilities is your master-teacher companion. Have you been taking notes or marking passages? If so, go back and reread them. If you've been underlining, skim through the pages you've read. Anything stand out? Any words touch you in the heart or leap off the page? Put any phrases or ideas or images that feel significant in your big pot, even if you don't know why.

Susan in Texas had a surprising encounter with a paradoxical possibility as she was reading her master-teacher companion *Care of the Soul* by Thomas Moore. In a chapter on the myth of Hera, Susan was surprised to read that "[j]ealousy serves the soul by pressing for limits and reflection." That sentence sparked something, so she went back and reread the chapter several times. Then she soul wrote about it at length and shared her conclusion with me:

> My need for intimacy coupled with insecurity regarding the sincerity/depth of a partner fulfilling my need has been festering all my life. Hence, I have a soul vow I never anticipated—"Accept Hera's jealousy as healing flame." Sounds like something to release, but in fact, it's the opposite for me.

Open Yourself to New Sources

At this stage of filling your big pot with potential vows, your wise, knowing heart might start directing you toward some new sources of inspiration. Don't be surprised if you feel pulled to go to an unusual movie or listen to a challenging speaker or attend a provocative play. Do you feel the urge to have a deep conversation with a spiritual director or soul friend? Is your car beckoning you to go somewhere? Pay attention. Remember, the soul takes nothing for granted—nothing. The smallest thing could be the perfect thing. Trust your intuitive senses to see words on road signs, hear phrases in songs, and capture ideas that come on the wind. Your job right now is simply to be open and receptive and gather all you are given. And don't forget to say thank you!

Masha in Texas told this amusing story in one of my Soul Vows classes:

> I had no idea about how I was going to receive my soul vows. I wasn't stressing over them. I wanted them to come

on their own. I went to Las Vegas to visit my son, and in a metaphysical store I suddenly decided to have a Tarot reading. The first thing the reader said was "step into your power." Those words stunned me; they pierced my mind and my heart. I don't even remember the rest of the reading. I felt like those words was all that was needed. I think the reader sensed that too, because she repeated it several times. I knew "step into your power" was my first soul vow.

Then a few days later, I read a quote by Thomas Keating and for some reason put the book down and went to look up Keating online. I read a review of one of his books, and the name Mary of Bethany popped out at me, and I felt an instant connection to her. When I went to sleep that night, without any real thought beforehand, I asked Mary of Bethany if she has a soul vow for me, and in the morning I woke with two words, *compassion* and *engage*. At first I thought, "*Engage* I can see as a vow, but *compassion?* I don't want compassion as a vow." But I couldn't get compassion out of my mind; it just wouldn't leave. It was attached to me, and I knew that it is one of my soul vows. And so *compassion* and *engage* became my second and third soul vows.

Pat in Texas didn't have to go as far as Las Vegas; she simply responded to a nudge to step outside. She shared what happened:

Last week, I decided to sit outside. My soul vows were not oozing up like I had anticipated. I admit I was not trying hard because I did not want to make up something that had anything to do with self-improvement. In my past experience, these attempts were usually short lived. I wanted something that was true and would last.

Across the street and two houses away, I saw a white bird. I hoped the bird would come closer. It did! It flew over my driveway and over me. I was quite taken that it came so close to me. I called my husband on my cell phone to come out and look at the white dove. It settled in the street for a few minutes for my husband to see it and for it to drink some rainwater out of a puddle before it flew off.

After its departure, I asked what the bird symbolized: peace. My first soul vow is "I live in peace." An angel reading confirmed that this was the meaning of the white dove and that this was my first and most important soul vow.

Pat found her soul vow in a beautiful dove. Your heart, however, may ask you to look at something that isn't so pretty, something that breaks your heart. Don't be frightened. And don't turn away. Your soul vows are leading you to *be* true beauty in the world. What breaks your heart holds clues to how you want to make a difference.

Gandhi is misquoted as saying, "Be the change you wish to see in the world." What he really said is deeper and much closer to the impact of fully lived soul vows: "If we could change ourselves, the tendencies in the world would also change. As a man changes his own nature, so does the attitude of the world change towards him. . . . We need not wait to see what others do." Your personal transformation and the transformation of the world walk hand-in-hand as you live your soul vows.

This is certainly the case with my son. Every one of his soul vows—honor the dignity of all, engage in deep inquiry, live in solidarity, and seek justice for those who cannot seek it for themselves—are ways he brings healing and beauty into the world. But before he could begin to help heal the world, he had to look at the pain and suffering around him and see it—really see it. And then, in his broken-open heart, he committed to do something whether others were willing to join him or not.

Fill Your Big Pot

Is your big pot getting full? Don't be surprised if you have dozens of potential soul vows in there. You will start sifting and sorting them soon, but don't feel any pressure to rush to that step. Wait until you feel content that your pot has all the raw ingredients it wants. There is no right number of items in the pot. No one can tell you when your big pot is full. But your heart knows. Check within. Ask your wise, loving heart if you are ready to go on. If you feel a smile in your chest or one blooms on your face, you are ready to meet your potential vows in a more intimate way.

Get to Know Each Potential Soul Vow

Before you can identify the precious values you want to embody for life, sit for a few minutes with each one in your pot and get to know it. You can do this by calling each vow by name in your mind, out loud, or on the page. I'm a big fan of doing this in soul writing because information and insights have a better chance of sneaking past your overactive conscious mind when you write. However you do it, the key is simply to be open and invite each one to step forward and speak. You called your critical voices forward and listened to them. You asked each false master to tell you its story and deliver its gifts. Now you get to have a conversation with each potential soul vow. And this time, there need be no trepidation. These conversations will be delightful, insightful, and fun.

So begin. Pick a potential vow out of your big pot. If you have them in an actual pot, close your eyes and ask your angels to guide you to a piece of paper. Look at the words on the page with love. Then address that value by name. Following the wisdom of three, speak its name three times, saying in essence, "I call you forward, I am open to your wisdom, and I am ready to integrate your wisdom into my being."

As the first potential vow comes forward, notice how it looks. Feel its presence, its personality, its warmth. Watch as it settles down beside you to talk. Then open a conversation. Here's an example:

Dear "I live in integrity,"
You are one of the most beautiful values in my pot. You have such a lovely name, and everyone says you are important. Please tell me more about

yourself. I'd like to know who you are at depth. Help me see what a lifelong dance with "I live in integrity" would look like. I'm open. I'm ready to hear you. I'm listening with my spiritual heart. Tell me what I need to know about inviting "I live in integrity" fully into my life.

As you write, listen—not so much with your ears or your mind but with your heart. When something resonates in your heart, like a bell tolling or invisible hands clapping, or your heart feels like it is expanding in size or warmth, capture what you hear. Underscore. Highlight. Mark the page. Speak the words aloud. Do *something* to capture the elegance and beauty with which that potential vow is speaking.

Don't be concerned if you don't understand. Often *not* understanding is the hallmark of a particularly precious and important vow.

And don't run away if something seems too big for you. The best vows are. These are the ways you gather the Presence of the Divine; how could they be anything but big? What seems enormous to your human self is just the right size to your divine Self.

One more thing: don't ignore a value that wants to be noticed. If something shows up three times, pay attention, whether you like the sound of it or not. A woman in a Soul Vows course told a story about setting out to mail a package. She went to first one than another location, but there was a problem each time. Finally she gave up and started to drive across town. As she merged onto a busy street, a delivery truck pulled alongside her. Emblazoned across the side in huge red letters were the key words of a vow she had been ignoring for days. She burst out laughing, "OK! I don't get it! But OK!"

Sometimes you may feel you don't need to have a conversation with a vow in the pot. That doesn't mean the value isn't lovely or important; it may mean you already know it well, or it has nothing new to teach you. Your soul vows stretch you into the very Presence of the Divine on earth, so if a value seems to be stepping aside, let it go. You may hear something like, "You don't need me right now. Let me go on to someone who does." When this happens, smile, say thank you, and release the vow from your pot. If you're uncertain, ask if there's a deeper iteration of it that would like to live inside you. Karen in New York said her familiar friend "Kindness" stepped aside so she could meet a vow that rattled her down to her bones, "I am the embodiment of Love."

When you have spent time with each of the values in your big pot, stop and take a breath. Thank them all for coming and ask if there's anyone else who'd like to come forward, anyone who's escaped your attention, any last vows who'd like to present themselves for consideration. Funny things can happen at this juncture. Barbara in New York said her cursor got stuck until she noticed the words it was glued to. Irene in Florida had to type in the answer to a security question when she made a mistake logging on to her bank account. The answer to the question held a huge clue to a soul vow. If a vow needs to get your attention, trust me, it will. All you have to do is listen once it has your attention.

Sort and Sift Your Big Pot of Values into a Focused List

You have a pot full of beautiful values, but you can't commit to all of them. Less is definitely more in soul vows. A short list of vows you adore—or in David Whyte's words "it will kill you to break"—has much more power than a long list of lovely attributes. You will affirm your soul vows every day—and not just in words. You will say them, yes, but you will also *live* them, which has a far greater impact. As you live them, you will find your world responding in a parallel dance until every aspect of your life is surrounded and supported by situations and people and experiences that mirror those same values. And as you live them, you will sprinkle these holy aspects of the Divine onto the world around you. In the end, you will *become* your soul vows, so you want to speak and embody a short, focused list of vows you deeply, deeply love.

People always ask me how many. There is no magic number. I have seven soul vows, and after I wrote them, I realized they parallel the seven chakras. Seven is a divine number, and I do love it, but your soul may have its heart set on five or six or eight. So don't start with a number in mind. Let the number be a surprise.

Don't go into this sorting step trying to make your vows match a system like the chakras or the medicine wheel or the zodiac, no matter how lovely or holy or good that system may be. This is not an intellectual exercise. Your soul vows are not a religious or psychological system. This is a mystical experience, a partnership with the Divine. The process isn't directed by your intellect, or your preferences, or your goals. Quite the opposite.

If you're itching to have a role, a part to play, a way to contribute to the creation of your soul vows, here's your job: Get out of the way. Step aside. Allow. Surrender. Trust. And play. Everything you need to know or want to know about how to live a life of wholeness, authenticity, and joy is coming to you. You have only to allow yourself to be gently and sweetly met by your precious soul vows as they rise to meet you.

Play the What-If Game

One way to give your soul vows room to be heard is to play the what-if game. What would life look like if you actually lived a particular value?

Look at your big pot. What value grabs you first? Take that value out of the pot (or select one at random) and write it at the top of a journal page. Consider looking up its key word(s) in a dictionary and thesaurus. You may discover nuances about the meaning of the words that spark something in your heart. Then start discussing that value in divine dialogue.

Here are a few questions that may help you explore the deep meaning and purpose of a value in your life:

Why is this way of being calling out to me?

What do these words mean? What do they mean to me?

How do I feel when I speak the words out loud? Does my heart leap in joy, jump in fear, or stay in neutral? What are my feelings telling me?

Does this way of being seem important to me? Why?

Is this way of being already in my life? To what extent?

Is this way of being easy for me, or am I struggling with it? If it's easy, does it belong in my soul vows? If it's not easy, is it trying to reach me or teach me something?

Is this way of being missing in my life? Is the lack of it a problem or a hole in my life? Is it important to me to rectify this gap? Why?

What does this value look like in the world? Do I want more people, situations, and things that reflect this way of being in my life?

If I were surrounded by people and situations that held this value as well, what would my life look like? Feel like? Is this how I want to live?

How would my life change if I walked the earth embodying this quality? Do I want those changes? Am I ready for those changes?

Can I commit to living this way? What scares me about committing to live this way?

If I asked heart if she wants to live this way, what would she say?

Sort Your Potential Vows

As you spend time with each of the values in your big pot, check into your heart and listen for guidance to help you sort them into piles. This is an organic, heart-directed process, and you are free to design it any way you want. Just don't make it too elaborate, or you'll slip into full-blown "I can control this!" conscious mind, weighing the plusses and minuses of everything and before you know it, you've put your intuitive self to sleep.

To stay in the flow of heart-knowing, sort quickly. Here are three simple sorting piles that have helped many begin to hear the song of their final soul vows:

I love this value. I can't wait to declare it and live it every day—*yes!*

I love this value, but I'm not certain it belongs in my soul vows—*maybe*.

This is a lovely value, but I don't think it belongs to me right now—*no*.

Speak each vow aloud and let the electromagnetic field flowing around your heart make a quick, intuitive decision. You can trust your heart. It has access to information your well-schooled, highly rational intellect does not. If your heart leaps with excitement about a vow, quickly add it to the *yes* pile. If your heart feels warm but not ecstatic, put that value in a *maybe* pile. If you shrug your shoulders, put that value in a *no* pile. When something goes in the *no* pile, that's not a judgment of the quality of that value; your heart is simply letting you know that you are not the one being called to embody it. If you can't get a read on a vow, but you don't feel comfortable putting it in the *no* pile, set it aside and return to it after your heart has filtered the others. Sometimes it takes a bit of practice to sense and fully trust the impulses rising out of your spiritual heart.

Here's how I reacted to saying "I live in partnership" for the first time. After decades of being treated as less than, one of my deepest desires was to attract only people who would treat me like a partner—a valued partner. And I knew on a deep, visceral level that to get others to treat me as a partner, I had to first treat everyone around me as a partner. When I said the potential vow "I live in partnership" aloud for the first time, my heart jumped on every word. It loved the personal responsibility inherent in the opening pronoun because I knew no one could do this but me. I had to step in and step up to my authentic life as a partner to all I meet. Next, my heart started humming on the verb. This is how I want to *live*—not just think about or occasionally remember. This is how I want to live morning, noon, and night. Partnership isn't something out there that I seek to find; partnership is who I am, and it emanates from me in everything I do. Last, my heart nodded a firm assent for *in partnership*. It even liked that little preposition *in*. As I spoke this vow aloud, I could feel myself slipping *into* a state of partner-ship and *into* a pool of wonderful, loving partners. I knew from the very first time I spoke "I live in partnership" aloud that this vow was for me.

Try it. Test them all out loud. Play with the language. Let the words move around or change altogether. Notice how your heart and body respond to a whole vow and to its individual words. You'll know when your heart loves a vow. There will be no doubt. You will feel your heart respond so strongly you'll think for a moment it might burst inside your chest. Tears will well up. You'll take a little involuntary gasp. All these clues are a full-body *amen*! When that happens, just accept the words and place that sentence into your soul vows list, whether you under-stand it or not.

When you're finished sorting, look at the vows in your *yes* pile with love. Speak each potential vow aloud, one after another, pausing a bit between each. Notice if some of the words want to change, and make those changes.

Notice how the vows sound as a unit. As you speak them, do a few seem to skip to the front? Do others get quiet or even ask to bow out? Usually at this point several vows step aside. This is a good thing. Your potential soul vows list has an energy of its own. It is a living, breathing, organic part of you. It is your soul on paper. So the list can and will arrange and create itself. As you learn to cooperate with your soul in this soul vows process, you're learning to live a soul-directed life in all things.

Embrace Spirit's Living Presence in Your Soul Vows

Thus far in your fourth-chakra exploration you've been enter-ing your heart to notice how potential soul vows resonate inside of *you*, how they feel to *you*. But soul vows are a partnership, and a divine one at that. Now that you know how to recognize the intuitive signals of your wise and beautiful heart, you are ready to use it to explore how the Divine lives in and around and through your soul vows.

There are two ways the Divine is present in your soul vows: partnership and Presence. The partnership piece is fairly straightforward. Once you know what you're looking for, Spirit's active participation in your soul vows will be easy to recognize. The Presence aspect is more mystical and mysterious and will take a lifetime to unfold.

Explore Divine Partnership

Let's begin with partnership. Long before I declared my soul vows publicly, I knew that my soul vows were a reciprocal partnership, and I could count on Spirit to help me bring them to life. That's why I labeled my vows "Janet's Covenant." I made a little chart to remind me of our covenant, but looking at it now, I wonder if I wasn't trying to remind God! Clearly, God needs no reminding. God is always beside me, guiding me to live my soul vows.

I say my vows starting at the bottom, with the first-chakra vow, so read this chart from one to seven.

Janet's Covenant with Spirit	Spirit's Covenant with Janet
7. Pray always	Shower me with profuse grace
6. Seek Truth	Lead me to the Truth
5. Surrender, there is no path but God's	Shine the light on the path
4. Come from Love	Love me
3. Honor myself	Honor me
2. Live in partnership	Send only partners
1. Unite to create good	Send the good and only the good

When I first began to say my vows, I would say Spirit's part, too. For example, when I said my first vow, "I unite to create good," I would add something like, "And I can do that because you send me only people who want to unite with me to create good." Or after I said my fifth, "I surrender, there is no path but God's," I would add "and you make it easy because you shine the light on the path so I can't miss it."

But sometimes, when I felt lonely and frightened, I would launch into an extemporaneous rant on Spirit's part. After "I surrender, there is no path but God's," I'd find myself shouting, "And you know what? I could use a little help here! I think I'm walking the path, but things are not coming together! There's *something* I'm not seeing, and I don't know what it is! *Please*, shine the light a little brighter, will you? Maybe you don't need a klieg light, but I do! You shine the light, and I will follow, but *you gotta shine it first!*"

Now, I know that Spirit did not need to be reminded of its role in my soul vows, and shouting was probably not necessary, but it made me feel better to blast out my confusion and need. At first I felt a little embarrassed about screaming at God, but then I read this totally delightful Hafiz poem. I felt it gave me permission to do a little shouting when necessary. (I highly recommend reading this out loud with gusto. If you're anything like me, you'll be laughing by the last line.)

Throw away
All your begging bowls at God's door,

For I have heard the Beloved
Prefers sweet threatening shouts,

Something on the order of:

"Hey, Beloved,
My heart is a raging volcano
Of love for you!

You better start kissing me—
Or Else!"

Hafiz, "You Better Start Kissing Me," from *I Heard God Laughing*, translation by Daniel Ladinsky

If a poet-saint like Hafiz can shout "You better start kissing me!" at the Beloved, I'm quite certain it's OK for you and me to do the same.

But before you do any shouting, asking, or even calm praying around your soul vows, it would be helpful to see the dynamic of the whole partnership, the whole agreement, the dual commitment. You want to look at not only your unshakable unbreakable covenant with Spirit, but also Spirit's unshakable unbreakable covenant with you. To begin to see that, take a potential vow out of your focused list and have a conversation on the page about Spirit's role in that vow. Your dialogue might begin something like this:

Beloved,

I am creating my covenant with you, and you know this is a two-way partnership. I commit to live a certain way, and you commit to provide the help, the grace, the support I need to live like that. If that is true—and I do believe it is—then I'd like to talk about how you will support me, love me, be with me when I commit to_____ (put in the full wording of the potential vow).

Have a conversation about all your potential vows and listen with your heart to what emerges. Take notes. Capture the ways in which your divine partner will dance with you as you embody your mystical marriage vows. Make a little chart if you like. But always keep listening with your spiritual heart.

Don't be surprised if you feel a rush of joy or tearful gratitude as you record ways the Beloved loves you. And don't be concerned if you don't grasp the full ramifications of Spirit's part in your covenant. You don't. You won't. You can't. I am still discovering, fourteen years after I first declared my soul vows, just how rich Spirit's participation is. It is an endless source of wonder and joy for me to watch how Spirit shows up every day in mysterious, paradoxical, and sometimes even comical ways. All I can tell you is Spirit more than holds up Spirit's end of the bargain. Grace truly does abound.

Cathy in Ontario kindly shared her covenant chart. Reading this may help you see some of the rich gifts in your own soul vows:

Cathy's Covenant with Spirit	Spirit's Covenant with Cathy
I am enough.	I hold you in my arms.
I remember the song of my Soul.	I sing your song so you can hear.
I nourish myself with gentleness, love, kindness, and attention.	I nourish you in all ways.
I shine my light so others can see. My voice is heard.	I amplify your voice.
I dance into the next space. I co-create with Spirit.	I open the next space for you.
I surrender to the Grace and Presence of Divine Love.	I am always with you.

Over time, as the universe responds to you living your soul vows, you will discover for yourself that the Sufi saying "If seekers take one step on the path, Sacred Unity will take ten steps toward them" is true. The proverb comes from this beautiful *Hadith* (saying) of Muhammad:

> If they remember me in their heart,
> I remember them within my heart.
> If they come toward me walking,
> I come toward them running.

from a *Hadith Qudsi* (saying of Allah through Prophet Muhammad), as quoted in *The Sufi Book of Life: 99 Pathways of the Heart for the Modern Dervish* by Neil Douglas-Klotz

Isn't that the sweetest and most reassuring image? There we are on our wobbly human toddler legs, and there's Spirit rushing to greet us. The image makes the heart leap.

Explore Divine Presence

As you live your soul vows, your life will unfold in ways you can-not imagine right now. But as lovely as that is, there is an even bigger miracle ahead. The big miracle of your soul vows is a mys-tery—a mystical mystery. I call that mystery *Presence*, and it is the second and far greater way in which the Divine is alive in your soul vows.

Presence changes everything. It changes what your soul vows are. It changes why they matter. It changes what you're doing when you speak them. And it dramatically changes what hap-pens when you live them. It elevates your vows beyond a healthy or practical or even blessed way to live into the very embodi-ment of the sacred. When you speak a vow, you sound as if you are speaking it *as yourself, for yourself*, but that's not all you're doing; you're also speaking it *for* and *as* the Divine. I call this the "new I."

I first discovered the "new I" while reading Kabir Helmin-ski's *The Knowing Heart* on a gorgeous Florida Spring morning in my backyard. I had barely begun the book when I read this sentence, "Our 'I' is our relationship to the world, and as long as this rela-tionship is characterized by a self and world, we are in duality." I gasped. Not because of the content of the sentence; it was seeing the pronoun "I" in quotes. I grabbed my pen and and wrote "soul vows brings a new I" in the margin. I stopped reading and stared off into space, transfixed by this startling idea. In that moment, I knew at a deep, soul-ular level that bypassed all logic or argument that when we speak our soul vows, we may say our individual name and use the individual pronoun, but we are *not* the only speaker. As we speak, we create a space in which the Divine is present *in* and *through* and *as* us, bringing our vows to life in our life.

I had to test this revelation immediately. I raced inside, stood in front of my oh-so-familiar soul vows, and spoke them for the first time with the "new I." I began, "I unite to create good" as I always do, but when I finished, I added: "I, the Divine, unite to create good in Janet, through Janet, and as Janet. After "I live in partnership," I added, "I, the Divine, live in partnership in Janet, through Janet, and as Janet."

With each successive vow, I felt the creative power of this new and bigger *I* rising through my body. By the time I said my seventh vow with the "new I," my heart had expanded to a size I'd never experienced before, my mind was reeling in recognition of a mystical truth, and my face was drenched in tears of joy.

Moments later, I sent this email to the members of the Soul Vows course that was in session:

> After saying my soul vows as a two-part covenant for years, today for the first time, I spoke a third and deeper revelation. I said my vows as I always have, but then I slowly said each vow *as the Divine would say it.*
>
> Things were going well until my fifth vow, "I surrender, there is no path but God's." I wondered how or why the Divine would say that one. I always thought Janet was the one doing the surrendering. But I said it anyway, "I, the Divine, surrender, there is no path but God's in Janet, through Janet, and as Janet."
>
> I was stunned by that. God surrenders, too! God is, in fact, the ultimate surrenderer. God is not the ultimate controller—although that was the God I knew as a child. God is surrendering in and through me to how life unfolds. I had to take a long, slow breath on that one.
>
> So I continued, "I seek Truth," and God said, "I, the Divine, seek truth in Janet, through Janet, and as Janet." Oh my. Finally, I said my last vow, "I pray always." The Divine smiled at that one, "I, the Divine, pray always in Janet, through Janet, and as Janet."
>
> I cannot say I understand speaking my soul vows for the Divine in and through me. I don't think that matters. This is not a prayer of understanding. This is a prayer of union—a union I did not know existed till today. This is truly holy prayer.

Please understand that just as you do not fully know how Spirit will fulfill Spirit's half of the covenant, you do not know—cannot know—how Spirit will enter the world in you, through you, and as you. That's the way it must be. The living Presence of the Divine is not something you can understand intellectually, and it certainly isn't something you can consciously will or manipulate or control. It just is. Presence is the gift of the Beloved to the lover and the lover back again to the Beloved. In *Immortal Diamond*, Richard Rohr describes this sacred marriage in the sweetest, most tender terms: "Only the need of a beloved knows how to receive the need and gift of the lover, and only the need of a lover knows how to receive the need and gift of the beloved without misusing such love." This is the true wonder and joy of your soul vows.

An exploration of the Presence of the Divine in each of your potential vows may be the final clue that helps your list sort itself down to a chosen few. Take a vow from your list and speak it aloud, first with your name and then with the Divine's. If a vow doesn't start with the pronoun *I,* simply add it. (You need not keep the pronoun *I* in your final vows. I do not have an *I* in front of each of my seven framed soul vows, but when I speak them, I say the pronoun.) For the Divine's statement, you can use the name of the Beloved that you use in your soul writing or "I, the Divine" or "I, Spirit" or any other name that sparkles in your heart.

Here are a few examples of how to speak a potential vow with the "new I" of the lover and Beloved. The first two are from my soul vows:

I, Janet, come from love.

I, the Divine, come from love in Janet, through Janet, as Janet.

I, Janet, honor myself.

I, the Divine, honor Myself in Janet, through Janet, as Janet.

One of Susan in Texas's soul vows is "offer compassion without strings inward and outward." To hear the "new I", she added the pronoun and said:

I, Susan, offer compassion without strings inward and outward.

I, the Divine, offer compassion without strings inward and outward in Susan, through Susan, and as Susan.

One of Wendy in North Carolina's vows is "breathe deeply."

I, Wendy, breathe deeply.

I, the Divine, breathe deeply in Wendy, through Wendy, and as Wendy.

Usha in Northern California shared this beautiful story of her experience with the divine Presence in one of her bilingual soul vows:

One of my vows is "I do *punya* with presence." The story of this vow began years ago during a dark night of the soul. In that wilderness, my soul threw me a lifeline. I heard the words, "Do *punya.*" I wasn't clear about the meaning, since my Hindi is not fluent. As I was gathering my soul vows, I remembered that guidance. I asked myself, "Is there a soul vow in this?"

I felt called to find my copy of the *Lalita Sahasranama: The Thousand Names for the Divine Feminine*. In the tradition of bibliomancy, I opened the book for guidance. The page where it opened had three names for the Divine Feminine, all beginning with the word *punya*. The odds of finding these names were three in a thousand. It also included a definition: "serving others is *punya*." This was confirmation for me that my soul vow is "I do *punya* with presence."

I asked my father, who is fluent in Hindi, what *punya* means. He said there are two ways to interpret it. One is to do good deeds, expecting a reward. The second is to do good deeds but expect no reward. I realized that when I say, "I, Usha, do *punya*," I am speaking from my ego self, which does good deeds, but frankly would also like a reward of appreciation and acknowledgment. When I say,

"I, the Divine, do *punya* without expectation of reward," that feels aligned with my soul. I love that God does *punya* through me and as me, without any expectation of reward. It tickled me that there was room in the word *punya* for my ego self and my divine self. This vow feels like a gift from my soul and a blessing from my ancestors.

Speaking each vow on behalf of the Divine, describing how grace flows in you and through you until it becomes you, is a very precious experience. It marks the first time you name the living Presence of the Divine in and through your vows.

Write the remaining vows on your focused list in this "new I" format in your journal. Leave room to capture whatever emerges as you say them. Then slowly and from the heart, speak your paired commitments. Listen deeply. Notice how your heart responds to the energy of the words. Feel grace flowing through you. Feel the Presence on your tongue. This is a holy moment. Savor it. Through it, your soul vows are making themselves known.

I, _____(your name), _____
(your potential soul vow).

I, the Divine, _____
in _____, through _____, as _____.

After you've spoken your potential vows this way, stop and simply rest in the divine embrace you just experienced. Put your hands on your heart and whisper thank you.

Experience the Mystical Marriage

From the moment I received the concept of the "new I," I began saying my soul vows in dual sentences, first as myself and then as the Divine flowing in and through me. This way of praying my soul vows made me very happy and felt complete. But my soul vows had one more surprise for me! One more door swinging open into an even deeper chamber of divine Presence.

Because my vows match the chakras, when I say them, I put my hands in front of each of my chakras as I speak each vow. One morning, I instinctively began to rotate my right hand clockwise in front of my first chakra as I said, "I, Janet, unite to create good." And then, without thought, I began to rotate my left hand counterclockwise as I said "I, the Divine, unite to create good in Janet, through Janet, and as Janet." I started laughing. This felt so good! With my two hands rotating in opposite directions, I suddenly blurted out, "I, the one who unites, is the one who is united!"

Oh! I stopped and stared at the framed soul vows in front of me. Could this be true? Could the two *I*'s, Janet and the Divine, become so close that there is no separation? Is there really only one *I*? Only one who? Could all the vows work this way? Could this be the third and closing way to speak my vows? Could this be the deepest truth of the sacred marriage—first me, then you, then *us*?

With a bit of trepidation, I quickly tried an "I the one who . . . is the one who is . . . " experiment. Here's how it sounded for my vows. To experience this as I experienced it, read from the bottom:

I, the one who prays, is the one who is prayed.
I, the one who seeks truth, is the one truth seeks.
I, the one who surrenders, is the one who is surrendered.
I, the one who loves, is the one who is loved.
I, the one who honors, is the one who is honored.
I, the one who partners, is the one who is partnered.
I, the one who unites, is the one who is united.

I confess that grammar flies right out the window when you speak this kind of mystical language. Even though the sentences make no sense—how can I "be prayed"?—they are nevertheless naming the essential truth at the core of my being. This depth of truth is something no one can tell you or give you—not even me. This mystical truth is beyond knowing or even agreeing. It is a surrender, a merging of the two—the lover and the Beloved—

until there is only one: "the one who." It is the consummation of the divine embrace.

You will get giddy speaking your soul vows this way, but do try. Simply take a vow and begin: "I, the one who _____." For your initial experiment, put the complete wording of a vow in present tense and active voice. As you speak it aloud, it may reduce itself to a key verb or phrase. Then finish your vow: "is the one who _____." For the second phrase—the consummation phrase—put your vow in past tense or passive voice.

If your vows quite don't fit this format, play with the wording until you find a construction that feels like it captures the ecstatic marriage at the heart of your soul vows. And don't be surprised if your new sentences blow your mind!

Here are a few examples:

Brenda's vow	"To dance in the radiance that I am"
becomes	"I, the one who dances in the radiance, is the one radiance dances in."
or	"I, the one who dances, is the one who is danced."
Belinda's vow	"I serve the Light"
becomes	"I, the one who serves the Light, is the one Light serves."
or	"I, the one who serves, is the one who is served."
Alice's vow	"I see beauty everywhere"
becomes	"I, the one who sees beauty, is the one beauty sees."
or	"I, the one who sees, is the one who is seen."

Masha's vow	"I step into my power"
becomes	"I, the one who steps into power, is the one power steps into."
or	"I, the one who powers, is the one who is powered."

Linda's vow	"I release judgment of self and others"
becomes	"I, the one who releases judgment, is the one judgment releases."
or	"I, the one who releases, is the one who is released."

Now explore the sacred marriage in your soul vows:

My vow	_____
becomes	_____
or	_____

You now have an exquisite set of three ways to affirm your soul vows. First as you, then as the Beloved, and finally as the sacred union of the two. You can, if you like, also speak Spirit's part with you in this covenant, in which case you would have four statements. At this point in my relationship with my soul vows, I rarely feel any need to remind Spirit of Spirit's part, but in your early relationship with your vows, you may wish to speak Spirit's part in the covenant.

Here's a three-piece format that emphasizes Presence and the sacred union in "the one who":

Me	I, _____, _____.
Divine Presence	I, the Divine, _____.
Sacred Union	I, the one who _____ is the one who is _____.

And here's the full four-part format. Saying your vows this way at the beginning of your relationship reminds you of just how rich and holy they are:

Me	I, _____, _____.
Divine Partner	And you, Spirit, _____.
Divine Presence	I, the Divine, _____.
Sacred Union	I, the one who _____, is the one who _____.

Write Your Soul Vows

After so many deep explorations, you can trust your heart to now identify the small group of soul vows that will set your soul on fire for the rest of your life. Just as the list arranged and rearranged itself, the individual vows may make a few adjustments in their wording. Linda in Washington, DC, thought her vows were finished, but as she was writing the final list, she found herself writing "I follow my guidance" as "I live my guidance." She kept writing and out popped "I act on my guidance." The third iteration became her soul vow. Within days she experienced the power of the verb *act on* as she found herself taking action in ways she'd never done before. She said the difference in the words looked slight at first, but the words knew what they were doing as they guided her to a much more powerful version of her relationship with divine guidance.

Some of the last-minute changes in your soul vows may startle you. Fear not. You are not in charge of the wording. Your soul is. Your mystical heart is. The Beloved is. As you allow the language to move, your vows will evolve into a sharply honed, perfectly constructed song of your precious ways of being.

Even though you have been playing with your vows for days, even weeks, and feel confident as you write your final list, the truth is you don't understand it. Even if you think you do, trust me, you don't. Over time, you will discover just how deep your soul vows really are. Years from now, you will have *oh!* moments when a vow reveals something about itself that you never noticed, even though it's been right in front of you through hundreds, even thousands, of repetitions. So don't expect to intellectually understand your vows or sign off on them as the "right" list. It *is* the right list, but your conscious mind doesn't, and can't, know that. And that's just the way it's supposed to be.

Trust your regal divine Self to recognize and call forth its beloved soul vows. Your job is just to affirm them, type them up, and commit to renewing them and living them every day.

How will you know which soul vows are the ones for you? Here are a few clues:

- They feel good. Your heart opens when you say them.

- They belong together. They look good as a unit in some way you can't quite explain, but they look like a precious poem or song or hymn to you.

- They feel complete. Taken together, the list makes a congruent whole. It may be impossible to define or describe this feeling, but you know, and you know that you know, that these are the ways your soul wants to live.

- You recognize them as your own; they were always written on your heart.

- They describe your full, authentic life and your whole and holy Self.

- They make you smile, laugh, giggle, and whoop for joy.

- They bring tears to your eyes.

- They frighten you a little. You know you are committing to a richer, deeper life than you have ever lived before. (This is a good thing. If your soul vows don't make your eyes pop a bit and your heart flutter in expectation and awe, they're not big enough. And you are ready to play big.)

- You feel safe, loved, and protected when you speak them, knowing Spirit is beside you always, taking exquisite care of you.

- You feel divine grace flowing in you, though you, and as you as you speak them.

- They vibrate with power.

- They didn't come *from* you; they came *to* you. They are a gift—a gift you'll be happy to open for the rest of your life.

- You love them. In the end, that's really the only criteria, you *love* them—and they love you back.

Then there's the final test: are they unshakable and unbreakable? Will it kill you to break them, as David Whyte said? That means if you broke them, you would stop being *you*. For example, if I broke "I live in partnership" by willfully cheating someone out of work they'd done with me, my heart would break, my soul would scream; I would literally feel sick to my stomach. I would not be the Janet who is treated beautifully by all her many partners, and I would not be the whole and holy Janet I am here to be.

I had a small and funny test of this last summer in the grocery store. When I started to unload my groceries into the car, I noticed an avocado that missed detection under my grocery list. My first thought was, "Oh goodie, a free avocado!" But my stomach had a different reaction. I sighed and pushed the cart back into the store. As I handed the clerk a dollar for the avocado, she stared at me. I felt like saying, "Honey, I know no one pushes a full cart across a hot parking lot for a lousy dollar, but trust me, this matters. I live in partnership. I live in partnership with everyone—even my grocery store." A week later an unexpected windfall fell into my pocket. I felt that was a little Spirit wink of partnership.

Alice in Illinois (she of "Dear Kat") thought she had six final vows. Then she reread David Whyte's poem and found it held several clues to her "True Vows":

The words "hold to your own truth at the center of the image you were born with" struck me. I thought how true this is that from birth we have carried our soul vows in our heart. As I thought about this idea and applied it to my life, I realized, of course, it would kill us to break our vows. How do we know? Because every time we do, we experience the pain of separation from who we really are, and we are thrown into the abyss of suffering the consequences.

I remembered the times that I was most unhappy were the times I was being "someone else." As my soul vows emerged, I kept hearing this little question: would it kill you to break this vow? Would you be unhappy, suffering, or lost in darkness without living in this way? I thought about past experiences when the essence of my vows might not have been present and how I felt during those times. I had six vows that kept my attention, but there were only three it would kill me to break.

1. I trust God always and in all ways.

    It would kill me to live without my divine partner.

2. I move in divine harmony and vitality and energy flow.

    It would kill me to not recognize the divine harmony flowing within the physical and spiritual experiences that make up my life.

3. I see beauty everywhere, and beauty nourishes my soul.

    It would kill me to not notice something beautiful every day.

    I'm sure these vows have been "at the center of the image I was born with." I'm also sure I have just begun to know them. How wonderful to think they have been with me from the beginning, always leading me to greater understanding and deeper connection to who I really am. I am so blessed to discover my soul vows.

When your soul vows announce that they are complete, write or type them on one sheet of paper and begin practicing the sound and feel and grace of your sacred union. When I printed out my vows for the first time, I put a copy on my altar so I would remember to say them as part of my daily prayers, but I also put a sheet on my nightstand so I would say them first thing in the morning. And I placed a copy on my desk to remind me to renew them before I started working. I also converted them into a screensaver and startled every time they showed up to remind me who I really am.

Sprinkle your personal spaces with your soul vows. And begin to say them—not once or twice but several times a day. Thus begins your beautiful lifelong dance in the embrace of your Beloved.

Fourth Paradox: 1 + 1 = 1

As expansive and exciting as the word *paradox* is, it almost feels too small to capture the mystical experience that just happened as your soul vows burst forth from your spiritual heart, carrying the truth of your sacred marriage. What was born of this union of lover and Beloved is greater than anything you have experienced thus far in soul vows and probably thus far in life.

Words may seem too small, but the image of a triangle does help us *see* the sacred marriage. The first leg of the triangle holds your human presence in your soul vows expressed when you speak the pronoun *I* and your name. The opposite leg holds the flow of divine Presence and grace expressed in the words *I, the Divine.* And then—oh! and then—the bottom line holds the two together, creating the perfect form of a triangle, as it carries the essence of this merging, this melding into one another with the startling truth "I, the one who . . . , is the one who . . ."

On the first triangle, you can see one example of this fourth-chakra triangle for one of my vows.

Take one of your vows and write it in its three iterations on the blank triangle: first you, then the Divine, then the union of the two. Or a different way to describe the paradox of the sacred marriage in words might be "I am, the Divine is, we are." Or perhaps

I, Janet, pray always in, the Divine, pray always in Janet, through Janet, and as Janet

I the one who prays is the one who is prayed

you'd like to use my little mathematical formula for the sacred marriage: $1 + 1 = 1$. That would make a head-scratching triangle!

What image illustrates the union of you with your Beloved? I like the ancient symbol of the overlapping triangles. Draw an image that feels like a symbol of your mystical union. When you are finished, sit with your triangle for a while. Allow the sacred truth of word and image to fill your heart with love.

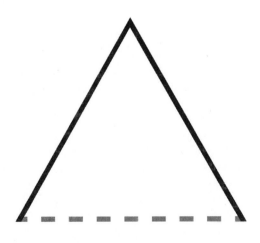

Fourth Discovery: I Am Open

What big discovery did you make during your profound explorations in this fourth chakra? You are carrying "I am ready" from the first, "I am free" from the second, and "I am whole" from the third. Those three discoveries prepared you to open your mystical heart and let it guide you to your soul vows. You became *ready* for this holy adventure, *free* from false directives, and transformed into a *whole* and empty receptacle for grace.

Do you sense how big your heart has become? We often say "my heart burst open" to try to convey the feeling of overflowing love toward something or someone. You now know that idiom is true. You heart did burst open—many times. It cracked when you realized your divine lineage. It expanded with the experience of wholeness. It burst with joy at the gift of your soul vows. And then it exploded in ecstasy at the incomprehensible gift of the sacred marriage.

If we had instruments that could measure the dimensions of love or the size of the soul, your numbers would be breathtaking. So put your hands on your heart and remind yourself of the truth: "I am open!" Then, in gratitude, tuck this fourth sweet discovery in your pocket. You will carry "I am open" for the rest of your life, as you turn to your Beloved every day in your soul vows, saying, "This is how I am open to you, this is how we are open to one another, this is how we are one."

Fifth Exploration

declare and celebrate your soul vows

Fifth Chakra: Throat Chakra
Fifth Paradox: To declare is to surrender.
Fifth Discovery: I surrender.

Within each human being is a vast Creative Power, a hidden treasure, but this treasure is not something we can possess. It is sweet, but it is not something that we can eat. By appropriating its qualities to ourselves, we short circuit the system. When we claim no qualities as our own, we will have the qualities of this Creative Power.

Kabir Helminski, *Living Presence*

Welcome to the fifth-chakra exploration and the most intriguing paradox yet: to declare is to surrender. The fifth chakra sings its paradoxical song of surrender right from hello. The lyrics sound something like this: To get what you want, surrender what you want. To receive, let go. To declare your will, surrender your will. Got that? Don't worry if you don't. Understanding will come, but it may come on little stealth feet.

The fifth chakra is the energy field that generates and supports communication and expression in all forms, especially speech. It's called the throat chakra because its creative powers emanate from the throat and encompass the mouth, nose, and ears. The fifth chakra vibrates with the creative energy of sound. In *Wheels of Life*, Anodea Judith says the fifth chakra is "the center related to communication through sound, vibration, self-expression, and creativity. It is the realm of consciousness that controls, creates, transmits, and receives communication both within ourselves and between each other. It is the center of dynamic creativity."

We know that speech has the power to create; our many creation myths tell us so. In the Rig Vedas, the Divine births the cosmos through self-projecting words. In the Judaic Bible, God said, "Let there be light" and brings the universe into existence with six consecutive "Let there be" statements (Genesis 1:3–31, *The New Jerusalem Bible*). The gospel of John opens with an exquisite ode to the power of the word: "In the beginning was the Word: the Word was with God and the Word was God" (John 1:1, *The New Jerusalem Bible*). Of course, we don't have to read sacred texts to know that speech can create. As preverbal babies, we figure out quickly that making noise gets us what we need.

Now, in the fifth chakra, you will learn the power of speaking your soul vows into being, your full self into being, and even divine Presence into being. Where does surrender fit in? That is the mystery ahead.

Deep Soul Explorations

In this fifth deep soul exploration in the fifth chakra, you will:

- declare your soul vows
- incorporate your soul vows into your daily spiritual practice
- immortalize your soul vows
- celebrate your soul vows with a ceremony

Declare Your Soul Vows

In the heart chakra, you met your soul vows, fell in love with them, and began to see how they carry divine Presence. As delightful as the adventure of *meeting* your soul vows has been, a far greater adventure—*becoming* your soul vows—is now beginning. It all happens here in the fifth chakra as you play with the creative powers of sound, song, vibration, rhythm, and full-body prayer to bring your soul vows to life.

Right now, your soul vows look like a short list of sentences, but they're actually a melody, a drumbeat, a chant, a dance. They are the song of your soul. If your soul vows are your sacred marriage vows and the way you embody aspects of the Divine, then your soul vows song is a most sacred song. But don't let the word *sacred* scare you. Just as your soul vows came forward to announce themselves, their sacred song will now appear in your throat. Your job is simply to listen and love what you hear.

Let's begin by looking at the elements of sacred song—breath, sound, rhythm, and melody—and then watch as they weave themselves together to create your unique soul vows song.

Breath

Breath is essential. Breath is life itself. That's why so many spiritual practices remind us to return and return again to the breath. In meditation, yoga, and many forms of prayer, we turn inside to witness the precious flow of life in and out on the breath.

But breath is more than the *physical* life force, holy as that is; it is also the means by which we receive the *spiritual* light of our own souls. From the moment I read the following passage by John O'Donohue in *Anam Cara*, the act of breathing changed for me. I feel so strongly about this holy partnership of soul and breath that I read this passage aloud at the beginning of every one of my courses:

> The soul is not simply within the body, hidden somewhere within its recesses. The truth is rather the converse. Your

body is in the soul, and the soul suffuses you completely. Therefore, all around you there is a secret and beautiful soul-light. This recognition suggests a new art of prayer. Close your eyes and relax into your body. Imagine a light all round you, the light of your soul. Then with your breath, draw that light into your body and bring it with your breath through every area of your body.

Take a few breaths with this awareness. See your own divinity, your own soul light, being drawn into every cell of your body. Notice how the tiniest recesses of your body vibrate in joy. When I do this, I feel my whole body smiling.

Breath also has another, even more amazing revelation for us. It comes from Richard Rohr's *The Naked Now*. I read this to all my classes, too:

> I cannot emphasize enough the momentous impor-
> tance of the Jewish revelation of the name of God. . . .
> As we now spell and pronounce it, the word is *Yahweh*,
> for those speaking Hebrew, it was the Sacred Tetragram-
> maton YHVH (*yod, he, vav,* and *he*). It was considered a
> literally unspeakable word for Jews. . . . This unspeak-
> ability has long been recognized, but we now know it goes
> even deeper: formally the word was not spoken at all, but
> breathed! Many are convinced that its correct pronuncia-
> tion is an attempt to replicate and imitate the very sound
> of inhalation and exhalation. The one thing we do every
> moment of our lives is therefore to speak the name of
> God. This makes it our first and our last word as we enter
> and leave the world.

Breath is truly holy, isn't it? And we have this divine Pres-
ence moving in us and through us every moment of life. Your breath will now carry the song of your soul vows up from your heart, through your throat, and into the air around you; then it will circle back inside you through your ears and nose and lungs. God flowing in; God flowing through; God flowing out.

When I read this section of *The Naked Now*, I suddenly under-stood the deeper meaning of my vow "I pray always." When I wrote that vow years ago, I remember staring at it and thinking, "Oh dear, that's impossible." But now I see that if I'm breath-ing, I'm praying. So perhaps it's actually the easiest of all my vows to fulfill! (Proving once again that you do not know what your vows mean at first, but you can trust them to reveal them-selves over time.)

I'd like to give Hildegard of Bingen, the great mystic and musician of the fourteenth century, the last word on breath. In her antiphon "O Quam Mirabilis Est" ("How Wondrous Is"), she calls out to the Beloved, praising all the ways the Creator gazes into faces and recognizes every creature. She closes with this ecstatic line: "What a miracle to be awake inside your breath-ing!" Oh, maybe we're not the ones doing any breathing at all!

Sound

On your holy breath, you make sound, and sound starts every-thing in motion. Emit even the simplest one-note sound, like *aaah* or *ohmm,* and notice how your chest vibrates, your throat vibrates, your vocal chords, your nose, your lips, your cheeks. You can't see the sound waves you are producing, but your ear-drums pick up the vibrations and pass them on to tiny bones and hair cells in the cochlea in your inner ear, which in turn send signals up the auditory nerve to the brain. The whole process of producing and hearing your own sound is nothing short of miraculous. In Hildegard's eyes, you have become a "singing pipe." In *Liber Vitae Meritorum* (*The Book of the Rewards of Life*), she writes, "[T]his sweetest blowing of the wind coming from the secret place of the Divinity touched these pipes so that they resounded with every type of sound that a harp and organ make."

Devi Mathieu began singing the music of Hildegard over twenty years ago. Intrigued by Hildegard's gorgeous composi-tions and the method by which they were learned, Devi began a deep study of the medieval oral tradition. She discovered that when we sing Hildegard's songs as Hildegard sang them, we can experience the divine connection Hildegard experienced. She calls this process "Through the Ear to the Heart."

Devi gave me a taste of this process on *The Soul-Directed Life* radio show. She began by asking my audience and me to say the first word in a Hildegard chant called *"Ego Caritas."* She told us *ego* is Latin for "I am a part of the universe." She invited us to simply repeat after her each time she said *ego* (*EH-go*), enjoying the back-and-forth without making any attempt at memorization. She encouraged us to feel the reverberations of the sounds in our bodies and feel the atmosphere created by the sounds around us. As we continued with this slow back-and-forth repetition, I noticed that after a while, I did stop thinking about the word and slipped into just being in and with the sounds.

Then Devi gave us the second word, *caritas,* Latin for "divine love and charity, limitless loving compassion." Once again, she had us simply repeat it and feel the vibrations of the sounds we were creating with our "pipes." After several minutes, she led us to say the whole phrase, *ego caritas,* but by then we were no longer trying to remember the words or think about their meaning; we were experiencing their essence in our hearts.

Try it for yourself. Take one of your vows and say the first word. Say it as if you are discovering it for the first time. Let your thinking mind rest while you immerse yourself in the sensory awareness of what's happening inside and around you. Feel the vibrations of the vowels and consonants in your throat, your head, your chest. Taste the word on your tongue. Feel the presence of the vibrations in the air. Listen to the sounds as sound. Become the pipe for this one holy word.

After you've said that first word fifteen or twenty times, couple it with the next word in that vow. Then speak the first and second words as a pair, and feel how you vibrate and how the air around you begins to vibrate in response. Keep adding words until you've said the whole vow many times. Notice how you feel. Notice how the sounds feel in your mouth, your chest, your nose, your ears. But most of all, notice how they feel in your heart. Now you know what it means to memorize something "by heart."

Rhythm

As you are sounding the words of your vows, do you find yourself naturally falling into a syncopated rhythm? Language does that. It's one of the ways we recognize that someone is speaking Japanese or Russian or French; there's an underlying pulse that we recognize even if we don't know the meaning of the words. Babies perfectly mirror the cadence of their mother's tongue. Listen to toddlers babble on and on. After a while, you can practically tell what they're saying by the bounce and fluctuation of their vocalizations.

Each of us has a distinct rhythm to our voice. If you recorded my voice but garbled the words, you'd still say, "Oh, that's Janet!" Instinctively you'd pick up the clues of my identity from the way I emphasize words and syllables, from the length and placement of pauses, and from the rising and falling speed with which I speak.

But humans aren't the only ones with rhythm. Listen to an owl hoot, a bird sing, or a dog bark. You can't miss the rhythm. Scientists hope to soon decipher dolphin communication from the patterns in the sound waves they emit. Mother nature has the best sense of rhythm of all. Her days to nights, her ever-repeating seasons, and her silent, slow rotation of the planets are all elegant rhythms. If you can, sit beside a shore and listen to the lapping of waves. Or sit in a forest and tune in to the dance of the wind in trees. These are the pulse beats of mother ocean, mother earth.

And don't limit your awareness of rhythm to sounds. Sit in a public place and watch people walk. This is a fascinating way to enter a person's being. Focus on one person; notice their posture, the cadence and speed of their stride. When you get home, walk to your door the way that person would. You will be surprised by how quickly and completely you can feel someone else in your body. Humans are wildly interesting, but watch the movements of lizards, grasshoppers, fish, and horses, too. I think you'll agree, *everybody's* got rhythm.

Well, if everybody and everything has rhythm, that means your soul vows have their own special rhythm, too. This rhythm isn't something you superimpose on your soul vows; it's something they invite you to notice. Speak your vows slowly, one after another. Start out in a slow cadence in a bit of a monotone. Let the words flow as they wish to flow. They will reveal their natural contours. The places where they want to pause or speed up or rise and fall in inflection may surprise you. The words may start tumbling over one another to say something special, or they may slow down to get you to hear something you've been missing.

An impulse to move your body in rhythm with the words may come, too. Initially it might be a gentle sway, or your arms might start to move, or you might feel the urge to tap your feet or clap your hands. I find my hands instinctively punctuate a vow every once in a while with a big, bold *clap,* as if my whole body is shouting "Yes!" Let the rhythm move you—not you move the rhythm. Your vows already know the dance; they are now inviting you to step in.

Melody

As you are feeling the natural pulse of your vows, you may find yourself beginning to hum. This is how Devi's husband, the composer Allaudin Mathieu, sets poetry to music. Whether he's working with a thirteenth-century Rumi poem or a twenty-first-century Gary Snyder poem, Allaudin begins to perceive the music of the poem by repeating a single phrase over and over again, a la Hildegard. Slowly the words reveal their natural lilt, and he finds himself intoning the words rather than speaking them. At first their melody may be just two or three notes, like a shy songbird disclosing her hiding place.

That's exactly what happened to me. After Devi was on *The Soul-Directed Life,* I stood in front of my soul vows the next morning, as if seeing the words for the first time, and asked if they wanted to be sung. I began to repeat my vows as Devi taught us. I said the words slowly, without thinking about their meaning. Then I began to hum them, at first all on one note, but rather quickly a little chant showed up.

Devi stressed on the show that Hildegard did not write her music as songs for performance, but as chants for personal devotion. When Rabbi Shefa Gold was on the show, she also talked about this difference. "Song is beautiful," she said, "but with chant, I expect to be a different person. I want to unlock the power of the sacred words and take them into my body." In her beautiful book *The Magic of Hebrew Chant*, she explains the difference more fully:

> A chant is different from a song. It is a meditative practice that encompasses and integrates our inner and outer dimensions. When I sing a song, I am communicating meaning and expressing beauty to the listener "out there." But when I chant, I am also communicating with and awakening places inside me that need to hear and be touched by the chant. A song may entertain, but a chant is meant to transform. When you've learned the melody and rhythm of a chant, you've only touched the surface. Then, you can begin to explore the inner dimensions of the chant.

Doesn't that sound exactly like soul vows? You are communicating with and awakening something inside you that needs to hear and be touched by your vows, and you've only touched the surface of what your vows are and how they are transforming you. No wonder chant is such a perfect way to declare your soul vows.

Not that you have to chant them. You may prefer reading them as poetry or reciting them as a litany. That's how Lily in Massachusetts says her vows. She repeats each one following the pattern of the Sermon on the Mount: "Blessed am I when I . . ."

Movement

In a Soul Vows class one night, several members talked about saying their vows in two languages and discovering new layers of meaning. I taught deaf children in my first career and still remember a modicum of sign language, so the next morning, with the help of my sign language dictionary, I slowly signed each one. The movement of the signs opened layers of meaning I'd never noticed before.

You could also select a mudra for each vow and move your hands in a hand-prayer as you chant or speak your soul vows. You can find classic mudras in the wonderful reference book *Mudras: Yoga in Your Hands* by Gertrud Hirshi, or you can create your own. Masha in Texas created her own left and right hand mudras. She speaks her soul vows first with her left hand for herself and then with her right hand for Spirit. As she finishes each vow, she joins her hands together symbolizing the sacred marriage.

If you're wondering how to begin, think back to the delight-ful kindergarten song "The Itsy Bitsy Spider." If you remem-ber, your hands are the spider, crawling up the spout, and then become the rain pouring down. That's a sweet example of hands telling the story of the song. An interesting discussion to have with your vows might begin with "*show* me our story."

You can also feel your vows in your whole body by bowing as you say each one, or turning to the four (or six) directions as you speak them, or dancing them in simple steps like the Dances of Universal Peace (dancesofuniversalpeace.org). Ask your soul vows how they want to be prayed, and they will reveal something holy and sweet that expresses your dual lineage and engages your entire being in a whole-body prayer.

Mantra

When you engage your whole being in praying your soul vows, the vows shift subtly from list to blessing to sacred mantra. The Eastern esoteric traditions have long embraced the trans-formative power of mantra, but as a Westerner raised Christian, the word *mantra* wasn't in my spiritual vocabulary—that is, until I stumbled upon this quote in *You Are Here* by Thich Nhat Hanh: "When you speak with 100 percent of your being, your speech becomes mantra. In Buddhism, a mantra is a sacred formula that has the power to transform reality." Well, I certainly pray my soul vows with everything I've got, and after fourteen years, I can attest that my soul vows have transformed my reality completely. So I wanted to know more about mantras and how they work.

In Harish Johari's *Chakras* I found exactly what I was looking for. He explains that in the Vedic tradition there is a sixteen-petal lotus at the center of the fifth chakra. Each petal holds a divine quality, and the petals flutter in response to the sounds in mantras, releasing the essence of those qualities. I immediately saw my own throat chakra as a seven-lotus—one petal for each of my seven vows. Then, as I chanted my vows, I could feel the individual petals flutter in response, releasing the perfume of my precious vows. What a beautiful explanation of how our soul vows gather the Presence of the Divine in us, through us, and as us.

Visualize your own throat-chakra lotus, with one petal for each of your soul vows. Then chant your soul vows, and feel the petals flutter and release a waft of the qualities your soul has chosen to embody. I think Hildegard would love this ancient awareness of what happens as we become the singing pipes for the breath of the Divine.

As much as you enjoy the way you and your soul vows pray together today, know that your prayer will evolve. The way I chant and sway with my soul vows today bears little resemblance to the way I used to "stand and deliver" years ago. The vows keep telling me what to do, and I keep listening. I sense we're singing in a glorious but slightly mysterious three-part harmony: me, the vows, and the Beloved. I have to pay attention to catch my part, but together we are creating a beautiful declaration of love that feeds me through and through and through.

Incorporate Your Soul Vows
into Your Daily Spiritual Practice

Do your soul vows fit naturally into your existing spiritual practices, or are you wondering when or where or how to renew your sacred marriage every day? My morning practice evolved gradually as each of the five things in *Your Soul Wants Five Things* found its way to me and added itself to the mix, until now I have a pretty clear practice that incorporates all five things, plus a few other prayers. I'll walk you through what I do and share what some members of Soul Vows classes do, and then let's look at ways to weave your soul vows into what you love.

When I step into my writing office in the morning, the first thing I do is smile. I know this sounds so simple, but I'm certain my little spontaneous smile is the first prayer of my work day. I smile because I love everything in this sacred space.

Smiling, I walk across the room and step in front of my creative altar, which is the top surface of a low bookcase. I stand barefoot on a traditional prayer rug I inherited from my ex-husband. I love this prayer rug; it anchors my altar and the entire office as holy ground. I take a moment to feel my feet on the rug and imagine my first chakra roots extending down into mother earth and up into father sky. Taking a deep breath, I light a candle on the altar.

As the flame comes to life, I look with love at my soul vows hanging directly in front of me. I chant them, swaying first to the left as my right hand rotates clockwise for my role in the vow, and then swaying to the right as my left hand rotates counterclockwise for the Divine's role. Then comes the really fun part. It took a bit of practice, but I can now rotate both hands simultaneously clockwise and counterclockwise as I chant "I, the one who . . . , is the one who . . ." I'm always laughing by the time I finish, but I'm also certain my soul vows chant clears and energizes my chakras, leaving me feeling whole and centered and ready to serve the Beloved all day.

Next, I put my hands in the air, and I speak my writing blessing. I wrote it seven years go, and the opening lines still set my heart on fire: "I am a writer. Today I write. I write of the divine connection, the power of the words, and the presence of Spirit. I write in union with and service to the only God. Grace abounds." My writing blessing takes about three minutes to say. I ring a little brass bell on my altar as I say the last line: "Thank you, God, for this day (*ding*), this life (*ding*), this work (*ding*), and these words (*ding*). Amen."

I then touch my son's picture on my altar and say the Perfect Prayer for him and for others, especially the members of the *Your Soul Wants Five Things* community.

I take a few steps across the room and stand in front of my Intention Mandala. It hangs beside my computer so it can feed me subliminally all day. I take a moment to align my heart with the center of the mandala, aware that I am aligning myself with the mystery at the center of creation, and then I chant a short litany of the six fertile conditions in which my beautiful, abundant life is growing. After I chant my first condition, "I am conscious intention," I intone my soul direction statement, "I, Janet Conner, use words to connect people to the light," and then continue with the rest of my conditions.

If you've been counting, four of the practices in *Your Soul Wants Five Things* are included in my morning practice thus far: to commit to values (my soul vows), to serve a purpose (my soul direction statement), to express beauty (my writing blessing), and to create life (my Intention Mandala). That only leaves the spiritual practice that started it all: soul writing. I'm not rigid about the order; sometimes, I interject writing in the middle of my practice, but usually I save it for last so I can leap up from my sacred writing chair and start bringing what I just received on the page to life.

Depending on how much I have to say—or rather, hear—in deep soul writing, my morning practice takes between twenty and thirty minutes. So imagine my delight when I read in *How God Changes Your Brain*, by Andrew Newberg, that "twenty to forty minutes a day . . . may be the ideal range of time to enhance the neural functioning of your brain."

I did not intellectually plan my morning practice. I did not follow anyone's instructions or formula. I would go so far as to say I did not create my spiritual practice at all; it created me. It's part of the surrender piece of this chakra. I surrender to my spiritual practice rather than design it or fix it or improve it. I *am* my practice. My part is to be present, open, and receptive. I show up. I am available. I pray. I feel. I love. I listen. And I am grateful. Somewhere in there, connection happens. Somewhere in there, guidance comes. Somewhere in there, comfort surrounds me.

You don't have to bundle all your practices into one time slot. I do bundle mine in part because they flow so perfectly, but mostly because I know if I say I'll get to something later, later never comes. If you'd like to chant your soul vows at a special time outside your existing practice, please do. Just don't be vague about the where and the when. Commit to some sort of spiritual practice. Because practice matters—and not for the reasons you may think. Practice isn't an obligation; it's your opportunity to experience a bit of surrender every day.

In *The Dance,* Oriah Mountain Dreamer tells us:

> We must find a way—a practice—that can take us to the emptiness and keep us there when we would run from what we fear it holds. Without this our lives become, not the graceful movement that dances awake who we are, but the stumbling sleepwalk or frantic running of those who are afraid because they have forgotten who and what they really are.
>
> A practice is a structured activity that offers us a way to consciously enter and be with the sacred emptiness at the center of our being. It is by definition done at a regular, preferably daily, basis. The regularity is what makes it a practice. You do it whether you feel like it or not, and not feeling like it—resistance—seems to be a pretty universal human response to doing anything on a regular basis, at least in Western culture.

Aside from writing, Oriah and I do not do the same things in our morning practices, but we do completely share the *purpose*. "At the heart of any effective practice, whether it is explicitly spiritual, inherently creative, or rigorously physical, is a structure that clears and holds open a space and time for slowing down and letting go," she says in *The Dance,* continuing:

> Letting go necessitates being with the fear that comes when we become aware that all that we love in the world—our very life itself—is impermanent. It can bring tremendous relief and rest to let go where we are trying to hold on, trying to keep the same those things which by their very nature are constantly changing. This does not mean loving life and the world any less fiercely. Loving well and living fully are not the same as holding on. But we cannot become conscious of where we are holding on, where we need to let go, without slowing down.

I love Oriah's description of practice. It sounds just like soul vows, for they help us love well and live fully, while letting go of all the whats and whys and whens of how the vows should come to life. Of that, we are not in charge.

I asked Usha (she of the "I do *punya*" vow) how she weaves her soul vows into her existing practice. She told me:

> My soul vows are part of my altar, in my office. Before I sit down to work at my desk, I stand in front of the altar and chant *om* a few times to attune myself to divine Presence. Then I chant my vows, holding my hands in *Anjali* mudra—prayer pose at my heart. This is a practice to dedicate my work as a divine offering to the world. I want to offer the best of myself in service to others and chanting helps me do that. As part of my spiritual practice I often do *Japa*—chant Sanskrit mantras. My soul vows have become an extension of my *Japa* practice; they are my mantras in English. *Japa* leads to inner silence and peace. After chanting my vows, I like to take a few moments just to be in the stillness. Then I sit down at my desk and get to work.

Alice in Illinois created a practice that leads to silence and ends with the anchor of her one soul vow:

When I originally did my soul vows, I had three that have since distilled into only one. I am an early riser, so I do my devotionals early in the morning, as the darkness gives way to light and the house is quiet.

I gather a cup of tea or water and sit at my kitchen table, looking out upon a beautiful hillside wrapped in nature's glory, no matter what season of the year. I intuitively choose an inspirational book or CD to nourish me, and I read or listen. Then I contemplate the soul of the author, and I may repeat a passage that catches my attention to get the fullness of the meaning. That takes me into the silence.

When I return from the silence, I express gratitude for this holy time, I say the Twenty-Third Psalm and my soul vow, "I see beauty everywhere." I think Kat taught me that even the parts of life we find unpleasant or upsetting reflect beauty. This one vow guides my life. It gives me the ability to know that I am beautiful, you are beautiful, life is beautiful, death is beautiful, and at the core of everything I encounter, there is always something beautiful. Even if I can't see it now, I know I will in time.

Marielle in New Brunswick has a lovely way of saying her soul vows from her feet to her head and from her head to her feet:

I painted my soul vows on an oval board, each one with a chakra color. I try to say them every day, but I'm not perfect on that. I light a candle to connect with God and Archangel Michael. Then I say each chakra twice. First I start with the root chakra, seeing myself doing it. As I say "I am grounded to mother earth," I see roots coming from my feet into the earth. After I've said my vows going upward, I say them again in "the Divine in me, through me, as me" form, going downward from top to bottom. I totally feel the energy while I say them.

Not long after I started saying them, my solar plexus vow changed itself from "I am kind and compassionate" to "I am kind and compassionate to myself and others." Wow. That changed my behavior toward me a lot. My food choices became a lot healthier. The respect for me got stronger. I guess I had always been kind and compassionate to others more than to myself.

At first I was maybe a little afraid of my soul vows, or nervous of the commitment, but now I trust them all. I say them with heart, and I mean what I say. They are truly how or who I want to be. I follow my soul vows with my Intention Mandela prayer practice and, believe it or not, I still say my Prayer Sandwich from *Writing Down Your Soul*.

Kim in New Jersey begins her practice looking out the window:

After everyone is out of the house, I go to my bedroom and sit at the window that overlooks the lake. I am quiet for about five minutes and let whatever thoughts come. Then I read the *Daily Word*, *Science of Mind*, and Alan Cohen's *A Deep Breath of Life* for that day and sit with those messages for a bit. After that I stand up and say my soul vows and then go to my Intention Mandala on my bureau and reflect on that for about five minutes. That's it. I am now at peace to start my day.

Lisé in Colorado chants in the ancient orthodox way:

My soul vows came sort of out of the blue when I had given up trying to get them:

I love, I attend, I listen, I hear, I learn,
I thank, I live, I breathe, I know, I speak

They haven't changed over the last three years; however, how I use them has. They are now part of a daily morning ritual that includes a spontaneous invocation, my soul vows, my soul purpose, chatting with the One about what's happening (talking, not writing), my conditions from *The Lotus and The Lily*, my creative blessing, an "out-vocation" or final benediction, and last, deep soul writing. In this ritual, I chant the various parts like an Eastern Orthodox chant during a liturgy. I learned to chant this way in my twenties, and it has stuck with me.

In addition to my morning practice, I chant my soul vows silently during the late afternoon walks I take on a trail near my home. I also chant them in the car, especially when I'm driving somewhere to speak. And right before I put on my headset for *The Soul-Directed Life* radio show, I repeat my soul vows, ending each line with "in Janet, through Janet, and as Janet *in The Soul-Directed Life.*" Soul vows are the perfect portable practice. You carry them with you wherever you go.

If you are new to creating a spiritual practice, or want to refresh your existing practice, begin with what you love. Is that devotional reading? Meditation? Movement? Going for a walk? Lighting a candle? Saying prayers you've said for years? Singing? Selecting an oracle card? Gazing at photos of people you love? Sitting beside a loved one's ashes? Choose one or two activities, even if they don't initially appear to be spiritual practices; if you love them, they are. Then weave your soul vows into what you love—or better yet, ask your soul vows how they'd like to be a part of what you love. You need not alter anything you already do; simply add your soul vows prayer to it or around it.

Or you can do the opposite: you can chant, speak, or dance your soul vows, and see what naturally develops around them. The actual practices are not what matters. What matters is that they are your own method, your own prayers, that connect you with your Beloved.

Just don't turn creating a spiritual practice into an intellectual exercise. You are gathering the Presence of the Divine in your soul vows, so that Presence can and will lead you where you need to go. It's that surrender thing again.

Immortalize Your Soul Vows

After you've lived with your vows for a while, a day will come when your heart and your soul and your entire body let you know the experimentation process has ended; your soul vows are now complete. Although your relationship with them will continue to evolve, the words themselves have found their form. For some people, this feeling comes thirty seconds after they download their vows. For others, it may be a month or two before their vows feel sufficiently cooked. Still others wait months for a final burst of energy from their vows, announcing they are complete. Whenever that moment comes, it's a signal to begin to imagine how to immortalize your vows. They are the richest prayer of your life and worthy of being honored in a special and beautiful way.

When I decided I was ready to immortalize my soul vows, I contacted a calligrapher. I did not give the artist a lot of instructions, in part because I actually didn't have an image in my mind of what the vows should look like, but also because I trusted her creative genius to work in concert with Sprit—and that's exactly what happened. I didn't tell her to add Celtic knots or capitalize certain words or use paper that looks like old parchment. Nor did I tell her to use dark purple, gold, or orange, but somehow

she intuited the perfect design and colors—as if she saw my writing chapel a decade before I did—and what she created still sings to my soul and lifts my spirit fourteen years later.

Other members of Soul Vows courses have inked their vows on fabric, painted them on walls, printed them on postcards, written them on mirrors, and even stenciled them on furniture. When Camille in North Carolina sent me a photo of her kitchen chair with her favorite soul vow painted on the back, my mind flew open to the limitless possibilities.

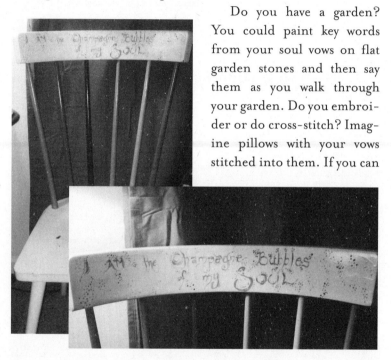

Do you have a garden? You could paint key words from your soul vows on flat garden stones and then say them as you walk through your garden. Do you embroider or do cross-stitch? Imagine pillows with your vows stitched into them. If you can weave or know someone who does, you could weave symbols or colors representing the vows into a prayer shawl or prayer rug. Even if you aren't crafty, you can get a fabric pen and a strip of cloth and create a prayer stole. I love the idea of writing them on a pillowcase and absorbing them all night.

A beautiful way to immortalize your vows is to make a necklace that holds their words or energy or colors and wear it every day over your heart. Another delightful option is to say your vows with prayer beads or malas. In the Vedic tradition, the finger-tips have a direct connection with consciousness. If you have any beading skills, make your soul vows beads yourself, imbuing each bead as you go with the energy and love of each vow. Or ask an artist to make one for you. That's what Lisé in Colorado did, and she was surprised when she opened the package:

> I got a mala with my soul vows written on small metal discs on one side and in angelic alphabet on the other. I allowed the artist to come up with her own ideas about the mala, and the result was awesome—especially as I never told her that I had just become open to the concept of angels. So it was one of those surprise things that was so right. But seeing my vows in angelic language sort of shocked me and brought tears.

Please don't think your artwork has to be elaborate. Lily in Massachusetts made a simple, joyful card in childlike primary colors. Even before I read the words, I started smiling.

Susan in Texas loves labyrinths. She goes to international labyrinth gatherings and has walked labyrinths around the world. She knew she wanted to feel her vows on a finger labyrinth.

When you suggested finding a way to move with the saying of vows, I immediately knew I wanted a dedicated finger labyrinth. I found an unfinished, pressed-wood finger labyrinth twelve inches in diameter with grooved circuits, and I decoupaged it with multicolored tissue-paper strips to represent sunlight on water, something that always connects me to Spirit. As the final layer, I pasted little stone images, one word per stone, into the grooved pathways, spelling out the vows with a bit of walking space between each. Then I shellacked the whole thing.

Now when I sit down to soul write, I trace my way into the center, reading aloud each vow as I run my finger over it, and at the center I say, "These are my soul vows." I stay "centered" a few moments and then begin writing. My vows labyrinth and my journal stay near my altar.

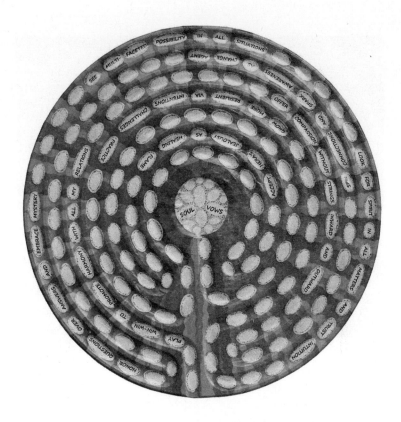

When I say the possibilities are endless, I mean endless. When Wendy in North Carolina began to live her soul vows, she realized her entire house no longer fit her. Over the next year, she repainted every room, creating an entirely new and bright color palette, but she didn't know what to do with the stairs. Fortunately, her soul vows did. In a dream she saw her soul vows written in a beautiful font on her stairs. The next morning, she searched online and was guided to a website with word decals. She opened a webpage, and there was the font she'd seen in her dream. When she sent me the photo of her finished stairs, my mouth fell open. It was the most amazing immortalization of soul vows I'd ever seen.

Have you noticed a theme running through these stories? They are all spontaneous, right-brain, creative surges, not logical, left-brain attempts to organize something perfect. And yet by releasing the desire to create something perfect, you create something that actually is perfect.

Here we are again getting another taste of the paradox of the fifth chakra: surrender. You've already discovered that your soul vows know their words, their song, and their dance. Now you have the delightful opportunity to discover they also know their creative expression. They know the form, the size, the medium, the colors, pattern, and materials. They even know who's going to make it. All you have to do is listen.

Celebrate Your Soul Vows with a Ceremony

After living with my soul vows for several months, I sensed something was missing, but I couldn't figure out what. I asked on the page in deep soul writing, and the answer was immediate. What was missing was the public declaration, the celebration, the party. I was reminded that all of life's major transitions are marked by gatherings. All through life, people who love you gather around you to celebrate your milestones. Well, I had just experienced something much more profound than graduating from school or moving into a new house. I had declared my soul's unbreakable, unshakable, sacred marriage vows—and I hadn't told anyone. No wonder I felt something was missing.

So I set out to create a holy celebration. I began with the date: November 11. In honor of the energy of eleven, I sent formal invitations to "Janet's Covenant Celebration" to ten women, inviting them to be my witnesses as I affirmed my covenant publicly for the first time. As they entered my house, I blessed each forehead with holy oil from St. Michael's shrine and said, "The Divine in me welcomes the Divine in you." When we were all in a circle on the living room floor, I told them the story of my soul vows, read "Bury My Dead," and gave each a small copper bowl so they could bury their own dead. Then each woman said a blessing for me. At last, I unveiled my framed covenant, stood, and slowly declared each vow. When I was finished, I put on a Mexican fire opal ring with the word *seven* engraved inside. My sister, Mary, and her partner, Mary'n, showed everyone how to lift and carry me around the room so I could see what it's like to be my "higher" self. Then we feasted on poached salmon and champagne.

The women were stunned. I was stunned. That evening really did etch my sacred marriage into my heart in a powerful way, and it was the beginning of a stream of 11-11 miracles that continues to this day.

There was something that happened that night that I want to point out in case it happens to you. Several women invited to my celebration were not able to digest what I was doing or understand how important it was to me. One even cancelled an hour before the celebration was about to begin. I was shocked. Looking back, I think many of my friends were more comfortable with the wounded me who needed them for support and less comfortable with the stronger me who was emerging. I didn't realize it at the time, but that celebration also marked the beginning of my new role as a writer and speaker. Half the women on the floor that night were not comfortable with this new Janet and gradually stopped seeing me. This hurt at first, but the vacuum was quickly filled with beautiful friends who resonate with my soul's values. Looking at the people in my life today, I see clearly that my soul vows really do attract those who mirror my values and deflect those who don't.

If you have a celebration, be mindful who you invite. This is not a standard-issue party. It is an ordination, confirmation, baptism, and sacred marriage celebration rolled into one. It is a commitment of the highest order. So take your time creating your event and considering who you want to be there. Ask your regal soul for guidance. Ask your vows if they want to be honored publicly and, if so, how. Ask your voice on the page for clear direction on what to create and whom to invite. Then create something beautiful, filled with meaning and joy. But know that even after you hone your invitation list, there may be people who can't come or can't understand how important this is to you. Bless them and let them go.

As you embody your soul vows in the first year or so, all your relationships will shift and move in response, and some may taper off or even end. This is not a bad thing. If you trust your soul vows, you have to trust their ability to rearrange your world. And rearrange your world they will. After living with her soul vows for one year, Marielle in New Brunswick talked about how much she had changed. She loved the new "Marielle 2.0," but found she could no longer tolerate commotion or small talk. The new Marielle was hungry for quiet and deep conversation.

Please don't feel any pressure to have a public ceremony. Every Soul Vows course concludes with a sacred circle ceremony, and for many members that is enough. When I ask the members if they're planning a public celebration, they often say their soul vows feel too intimate and holy to share outside the circle of fellow deep soul explorers. Usha in California did have a ceremony, but she invited just two—herself and Spirit. She spoke her vows and gave herself a gold ring, which she puts on occasionally when she feels the need. I do the same with my fire opal ring of *seven*. I wear it on very special occasions and always at our Soul Vows course closing ceremony.

Fifth Paradox: To Declare Is to Surrender

The paradox "to declare is to surrender" has been walking beside you from the moment you opened the door of the fifth chakra. Is it starting to make sense? Is surrender becoming your friend? There's a space between declaring your vows and surrendering to your vows, but that space is a mystery. That's why it's a paradox. The 2.0 version of you is being birthed in that space. So the best sentence I can come up with to describe what is emerging out of the union of "I declare" and "I surrender" is "I become." This makes me laugh, because I don't know what I am becoming! My fourteen-year history with my soul vows has proven that to me. But if this is where my soul vows have carried me thus far, I am ready and willing to let them carry me further.

This is what I'm learning about surrender: I am not in charge, but I can trust that what I am becoming—Janet 2.0, maybe even 3.0—is divinely guided and blessed. So I wrote "I become" on the third leg of my fifth-chakra triangle. What are you going to write? If words don't spring to mind immediately, take this question to the page in deep soul writing: *what is happening in the space between "I declare" and "I surrender"?*

Perhaps you will get an image to put in the center of your triangle, too. Now there's an interesting question: *what does surrender look like?* I got my answer when I read the poem "To Eros" by John O'Donohue in *To Bless the Space Between Us.* Here's an excerpt:

> May you be able
> To let yourself fall
> Into the ocean rhythm,
> Unfolding ever more
> Until you become
> One crest of wave,
> Rising into wild foam

So I drew a wave—a big wave that simultaneously lifts and carries me while washing me away. Pretty good image for surrender, don't you think?

Now it's your turn. This paradox is even more complex than the ones before, so take your time exploring the magical space between "I declare" and "I surrender." Perhaps the perfect phrase or image of the birth of you 2.0 will emerge.

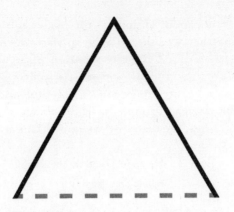

Fifth Discovery: I Surrender

I've been dancing with surrender for a long time because it's one of my vows—and the one I've wrestled with the most. For a long time, I'd grit my teeth when I said, "I surrender, there is no path but God's." But when the "new I" came, and I said, "I, the Divine, surrender, there is no path but God's in Janet, through Janet, and as Janet," I felt a rush of love for the mystery of surrender open up in me. Even God surrenders. In fact, God surrenders *in me*. Think of that!

I can't say I understand exactly what surrender means, though. I think surrender eludes definition because it is so personal. It is the experience of each individual at the heart of his or her own sacred marriage. Just as in human sexuality, you can't experience the sweet rush of communion until you surrender into the experience; so it is in the sacred marriage. No one can tell you what it means to surrender, yet I'm certain it is the key to a life of true peace and lasting joy.

The mystics knew a thing or two about surrendering to the Beloved, so I started hunting through Daniel Ladinsky's many books of mystical poetry, looking for the perfect poem to articulate this ecstasy of surrender. Then I thought, wait a minute, why don't I just ask Daniel? Here's his charming answer, with a fresh translation of a Hafiz poem just for readers of *Soul Vows*:

I like this one about Union, as the reader sort of has to piece it together, and then has the satisfaction—like working a puzzle. Also, I like the mention of a "wonderful game." Often good to un-serious-ize some of this God stuff—a prerequisite to Union, I bet. But also, this is remarkably deep and simple, as Hafiz always is. Plus, the more God sings, the better off we munchkins are!

> There is a Wonderful Game we should play
> and it goes like this:
>
> We hold hands and look into each other's eyes
> and scan all the holy regions of the Heart.
> Then I (God) sings, "Now, tell me a difference
> between us. And there is nothing, nothing you
> can say."
>
> Hafiz, rewritten excerpt from "There Is a Wonderful Game,"
> from *I Heard God Laughing,* translation by Daniel Ladinsky

So now Daniel and I—and surely Hafiz—invite you to write your own mystical poem about surrender. Ask your divine partner provocative questions like:

Am I sinking into surrender or holding back—surfing the crest or paddling hard?

Have I had a taste of surrender? What does it taste like?

Does surrender come bearing gifts? What are they?

How are my soul vows carrying me into surrender?

What would happen if I let Spirit play the "wonderful game" with me?

If I wrote a poem about my own "wonderful game," what would it say?

Then, put your fifth-chakra discovery "I surrender" in your pocket. Tuck in your own version of the "wonderful game" too, and join me as we gather the Presence of the Divine in the sixth chakra.

Sixth Exploration

gather the presence of the divine

Sixth Chakra: Third-Eye Chakra
Sixth Paradox: I know that I know; I know that I don't know.
Sixth Discovery: I trust.

Presence can offer us a continual relationship with Being. This continual presence merges into God's presence; it is the same presence. Awareness of the presence of God inclines us to submission and love.

Kabir Helminski, *The Knowing Heart*

Each individual expresses and incarnates a different dimension of divinity.

John O'Donohue, *Eternal Echoes*

You enter the sixth-chakra exploration with your beautiful soul vows in your hands and your special way of praying them in your body. You've woven them into your spiritual practices and into your days. Now, in the sixth chakra, you will weave them into your entire life.

At this moment you may think you know what your soul vows mean and what they can do, but as you live them, your awareness will expand and shift and, once in a while, take a logarithmic leap. Your soul vows will reveal new meanings in ways you cannot now foresee. And they will carry you places you cannot now imagine. This is the great and glorious dance with the Presence of the Divine.

This radiant dance comes to life here in the sixth chakra, the chakra of light. Even before you begin your exploration of this chakra, you can get a peek of that light with your third eye. Simply step into your cave of solitude, and when you are still and centered, close your outer eyes and look within your forehead. You will notice a glow of white and gold light flowing into your being through the center of your forehead and out again into the world. This light is the wisdom and grace of the Divine. You have this light. You've always had this light. You may not have tuned into it very often or learned to lean on it, but it's always been there, waiting to invite you to dance. Now, in this profound exploration in the sixth chakra, you will not only begin to see that light, love that light, and dance with that light; you will also *become* the light. That's what happens when you dance with light!

The sixth chakra is also the chakra of knowing. *Knowing* here does not mean retrieving information you studied, like knowing answers on a test. This is knowing at a much deeper level, and this knowing often arrives without you understanding why or how you know something—and yet you are certain you do. We call this *claircognizance*, or "clear knowing." But *how* does the sixth chakra know? And *what* does it know? In *Chakras*, Harish Johari tells us the sixth chakra contains "the eye of the I-consciousness, the organ of clairvoyance, the eye that sees all three divisions of time—past, present, and future." Meister Eckhart described this all-time-in-one-time in his Twentieth Sermon: "For the now in which God created the first human being and the now in which the last human being will fade away, and the now in which I am speaking—all these nows are alike in God and are only *one* now." I imagine Meister Eckhart was a deep student of Ecclesiastes 3:15: "What is, has been already, what will be, is already" (*The New Jerusalem Bible*). Is clear knowing—claircognizance—the breaking of the veils of time? I think so. And our soul vows, which also break the veils of time, help us do that and trust that.

One reason we struggle to understand light and knowing in the sixth chakra is that in the West we use two different words for them, so we tend to think of light and knowing as two different things. But in the East, they're woven inextricably together. In *The Hidden Gospel,* Neil Douglas-Klotz invites us into a Middle Eastern understanding of light that we miss in English translations of the Bible. In the phrase from Genesis that we looked at in the fifth chakra, "Let there be light and there was light," Douglas-Klotz points out that the Hebrew word for light—*aor*— refers to "all varieties of illuminating intelligence." There's that interweaving of light and knowing. If that weren't exciting enough, there's a big linguistic surprise in that sentence. The Hebrew word translated as "let there be" is the same word translated as "there was." That means the veil between future, past, and present must be very thin.

This union of time is an exciting and important paradox for us because our soul vows hold that same simultaneous flow of *now* and *then* and *will be*. In the "Welcome," I said our soul vows break the space-time barrier and call in your divine Self in all its expressions, past, present, and future. When you read that, you may have skipped over it because at the time it made no sense. But now, it is beginning to not just make sense, but it is also beginning to be real.

Douglas-Klotz explains this expanding awareness: "If 'light shall be' also means 'light was,' then in some sense the call of the future ignites the reality of the past in the opportunity of the present." Imagine that! The call of your soul vows, coming to you from the future self you are becoming as you live them, simultaneously flows back to you in unseen mystical waves, transforming not only who you are at this moment, but also who you have been in the past and who you are becoming. It's an endless circle of all time in this time.

If you feel a little vertigo reading that sentence, don't worry. Your soul vows know who you are. They knew who you were before you knew what they were. And they know who you are becoming as, day by day, the living Presence of the Divine fills you with light and knowing and spreads out into the world in and through you. It's a thrilling mystery, isn't it? And, wonder of wonders, it's alive in you.

Deep Soul Explorations

In this sixth deep soul exploration in the sixth chakra, you will:

- gather the Presence—light and knowing—of the Divine
- become the swan
- trust the dance
- be the light

Gather the Presence—Light and Knowing— of the Divine

Now that you are practicing your soul vows, not just as a prayer, but also as a total way of being, do you see why it was so impor-tant in the fourth chakra to embrace just a few vows from the vast field of possibilities? I like to imagine the Divine as a giant, radiant jewel with light pouring out of each facet. Each facet is one divine expression or quality or soul vow. I think this image came to me because I love this *Hadith* (saying of Muhammad): "I was a hidden treasure and wanted to be known" (from *In Search of the Hidden Treasure* by Pir Vilayat Inayat Khan). It's amazing to me that as I live my seven soul vows—and you live yours—we play a part in revealing this hidden treasure.

If we could add up all the soul vows being expressed on the planet, who knows the number we would reach. Humanly, no one person can embody all the divine qualities. No one person can radiate all the light of all the facets. And we don't have to. Each of us is called to embody just a few. But when I live my seven soul vows, and Alice lives her one, Lisé her ten, Susan her eight—and all of us are joined by *you* as you live yours—collectively we create a radiant jewel shimmering with divine light. I find this image comforting because it reminds me I only have to embody the light that is mine to embody. And I find it thrilling because in this image I see myself as one small piece of the diversity that is the unity of all. It is such a joy to see myself as one ray of the mystical body of the One.

Jesus explained our individual roles in revealing the treasure of the Divine this way: "Your light must shine in people's sight, so that seeing your good works, they may give praise to your Father in heaven" (Matthew 5:16, *The New Jerusalem Bible*). That's the English translation. To grasp what a first-century Aramaic-speaker Palestinian heard, let's turn to Neil Douglas-Klotz in *Blessings of the Cosmos*:

> Hearing this blessing of permission with Aramaic ears, we find Yeshua showing what happens when the light of our becoming—a tangible sense of our personal "I am" connects to the sacred "I Am" and allows itself to shine. First, we bless those around us by reminding them subconsciously that there is a greater reality to which we are all connected. Second, we bless our own inner self . . . this part of our being feels the weakness and fragility of human life. When we allow . . . our connection to the divine to pour through us . . . we feel a more expanded, connected sense of divine Self. The individual "I am" comes into contact with the divine "I Am."

We know this "I Am"! We recognize this "I Am"! It is the "new I."

Scholars love to argue about whether Jesus actually said something recorded in the Bible, but one saying they agree on is, "No one lights a lamp and puts it in some hidden place or under a tub; they put it on the lamp-stand ["candle stick" in some translations] so that people may see the light when they come in" (Luke 11:33, *The New Jerusalem Bible*). Yeshua uses the practical reality of crowded homes and expensive lamp oil in first-century Palestine to point to a greater truth. In *The Hidden Gospel*, Douglas-Klotz explains that the Aramaic words for lamp or candle all come from one verb root that means "to be illuminated, imagine, or dream. The word's roots point to a visionary state in which a person's boundaries or sense of self may expand greatly." *Light* used this way certainly sounds like clairvoyant knowing, doesn't it?

Douglas-Klotz also decodes the words translated as "light," "hidden place," and "tub" and concludes that Yeshua is giving us a succinct parable about being generous with our "intellectual and spiritual light." When you receive a vision, an awareness, a knowing—in Aramaic terms, an illumination—you allow it to permeate you completely, and then you generously share that light. In this way you "embody the light fully and put it into practice." Isn't that exactly what we're doing when we live our soul vows? We allow our soul vows to permeate us fully, then we radiate our chosen facets of light and share them generously with the world.

This generosity is not just a lovely idea; it's an obligation—or at least that's what Buckminster Fuller was told. When he was thirty-two, his life appeared to be in shambles. His three-year-old daughter had died, possibly because his family's house was so cold and drafty, and he'd lost his job and his savings. He began drinking heavily and considering suicide so the family could get his life insurance. The story of what happened next is recounted in *Buckminster Fuller's Universe: His Life and Work* by Lloyd Steven Sieden. As Buckminster Fuller walked along the shore of Lake Michigan, contemplating suicide, he suddenly felt as though he were suspended several feet above the ground in a white sphere of light. A voice clearly said:

From now on you need never await temporal attestation to your thought. You think the truth. You do not have the right to eliminate yourself. You do not belong to you. You belong to the Universe. Your significance will remain forever obscure to you, but you may assume that you are fulfilling your role if you apply yourself to converting your experiences to the highest advantage of others.

The voice gave Buckminster Fuller two revelations that are in alignment with our soul vows. The first is "You do not belong to you. You belong to the Universe." This is more than a spiritual metaphor; it's a scientific fact. Every atom now in your body was created in the giant furnace of nuclear fusion after the Big Bang. You are made of stardust. So it's true, you *do* belong to the universe. But also consider "You belong to the Universe" in light of how you gather divine Presence into your being through your soul vows and then radiate that Presence out into the world, shining the facets of the Divine that are yours to express. Yeshua's exhortation "Your light *must* shine" suddenly makes a lot of sense.

Buckminster Fuller took the command to seek "the highest advantage of others" very seriously. He devoted the rest of his life to envisioning a future that would work for all. His light shone so brightly that he is considered one of the greatest minds of our time. But your light and my light must shine brightly, too. We are each one facet of the whole, and the whole cannot be the whole without all of us.

There's a second statement in Fuller's clairaudient revelation that I hope you caught, because it's true for you, too. The voice told Fuller, "You need never await temporal attestation to your thought. You think the truth." Really? You simply *think* the truth? We can look at Buckminster Fuller's visionary inventions and see that he did indeed think scientific truths decades before the rest of us, but how is that possible? How did he think truths that weren't known to anyone else at the time? And can we "think the truth," too?

The ancient Vedic tradition can help us understand this mystery. In *Chakras* we learn that as we enter the sixth chakra, light forms around our head and around our body in our aura. As we meditate deeply on this chakra of light, we become a divine manifestation, revealing the Divine within, and reflecting the divinity of others. That sounds like soul vows—my soul vows reveal the Divine in me and reflect the Divine in you. Harish Johari explains that if we stay in this state long enough, duality simply fades away, and we become *sat,* which is Sanskrit for "true." Caroline Myss picks up this theme of truth in *Anatomy of the Spirit.* She announces in no uncertain terms that the sacred truth of the sixth chakra is "seek only the truth."

In Buckminster Fuller's case, it sounded like the truth wasn't something he needed to seek outside; it was already complete inside him. His thoughts already were true. Is this possible for us?

Become the Swan

The swan holds the answer to that question. Three years ago, I "saw" the covers of all my books in the *Your Soul Wants Five Things* series. *Soul Vows* had a swan on the cover. At the time, I didn't understand why a swan would be the perfect icon of this sixth-chakra exploration.

There are very few animals in Harish Johari's *Chakras,* so imagine my surprise when I read that in the sixth chakra, when the mantra *Soham* (Sanskrit for "that I am") is repeated, the syllables reverse themselves to *Hamsa,* the word for swan. Suddenly I was hungry to know all about swan, but Johari only added that swan "can fly to places unknown to ordinary people." I wanted more, so I jumped out of my chair to get two resources I love, *Animal Speak* by Ted Andrews and *Medicine Cards* by Jamie Sams and David Carson.

Swan's story in *Medicine Cards* is the story of grace. As a young gangly duckling, she was trying to find an entrance to the future, but all she could see was a swirling black hole above Sacred Mountain. So she asked a dragonfly what it takes to enter the doorway to other worlds. The dragonfly told her she must be willing to accept Great Spirit's plan as it is written. Swan replied, "I will *surrender* to the flow of the spiral and *trust* what I am shown" (original and very significant italics). She entered the black hole and returned—as she does in so many folktales—a graceful, gorgeous swan. The dragonfly was stunned at her transformation and asked what happened. Swan said, "I learned to surrender my body to the power of Great Spirit and was taken to where the future lives. I saw many wonders high on Sacred Mountain and because of my faith and my acceptance I have been changed, I have learned to accept the state of grace." The chapter ends with the reminder that when Swan appears, she is calling you to "accept your ability to know what lies ahead." Well, thanks to the totem of the sixth chakra, Swan has now appeared to all of us. And her medicine sounds just like Buckminster Fuller's knowing.

In *Animal Speak,* the section on swan opens, "The swan is one of the most powerful and ancient of totems." A swan, Ted Andrews reminds us, is a bird, and birds are always symbols for the soul. But the long, graceful neck of the swan has a particular symbolic meaning. The neck in any creature is a bridge. Think of your own neck bridging your body, representing the lower realms and lower chakras, and your head and its higher realms and higher chakras. "In the swan totem, as you begin to realize your own true beauty, you unfold the ability to bridge to new realms and new powers," says Andrews.

Is this resonating with you? As you embrace your soul vows and enter into the cosmic dance with the Presence of the Divine, are you discovering just how beautiful you are? As you live your soul vows are you becoming aware of yourself as a bridge between heaven and earth? Are powers of perception, awareness, and knowing starting to show up unannounced? These are just a few of the many gifts of soul vows.

Ted Andrews ends his section on swan by saying, "The swan is the totem of the child, the poet, the mystic, and the dreamer." When I read this sentence, I sat with it for a moment, and I suggest you do the same. I asked myself, "Am I a child? A poet? A mystic? A dreamer?" Well, I do feel more and more like a child as I live with my soul vows; everything has become a source of amazement and wonder. And I do find myself relying more and more on mystical poetry; nothing else seems to capture the relationship of the soul and the sacred. Does that make me a mystic? I wouldn't say that I am a mystic just yet, but I would say I am becoming one. And I think you are, too. Does that make us both dreamers? In English we often use that term pejoratively to mean not realistic, foolish, disconnected from reality. But in the Jungian world and the Vedic tradition, dreams are the playground of the soul. So my vision three years ago was correct. The perfect totem for soul vows is the swan because through our soul vows we become a living link between dimensions. We become the walking Presence of the Divine on earth.

I loved all I learned in the *Medicine Cards* and *Animal Speak*, but I sensed swan had even more to tell me. I looked around at my books and intuitively reached for *The Upanishads*, the oldest of the Vedic treasures and a sacred text I'm just beginning to study. It is thought the Upanishads were assembled as early as the sixth century BCE. *Upanishads* means "sitting down near." In their name, you can hear that these are the essential teachings a master would convey in story form to a student. I opened the book.

Instinctively, I was led to the Chandogya Upanishad. It tells the story of a poor boy, Satyakama, who asks a great master to allow him to become a disciple. The great master tells Satyakama to tend four hundred sickly cows. The boy vows he will not return until the herd has grown to a thousand healthy cows. When the herd is restored, the bull of the herd asks the boy if he'd like to know the four feet of Brahman (the Self). Oh yes, please, the boy says. So the bull tells Satyakama one of the four feet of Brahman—the four directions—and then says, "Fire will tell you more."

The next night the boy builds a fire, and fire teaches him the second foot—earth, sky, heaven, and ocean—and ends by saying, "A swan will tell you more." The next day, sure enough, a swan arrives and asks the boy if he'd like to learn the third foot of the Self. The boy says yes please, and the swan says, "There are four quarters: fire, the sun, the moon, and lightning. These make one foot of Brahman, called Full of Light. To meditate on this fourfold foot of truth is to be filled with light in this world and master the world of light." Then the swan says the last piece will come from a diving bird, and indeed it does.

After receiving these four teachings, Satyakama returns to his master, and his master recognizes him because he is "glowing like one who has known the truth" ("The Chandogya Upanishad," *The Upanishads*, translation by Eknath Easwaran).

I have been floored by how much the swan has to teach us! I wanted to know how the swan and the light and knowing of the sixth chakra work in and with people who are living their soul vows, so I called four women who took the Soul Vows course during the three years before I wrote this book. Here are their stories.

Joy

Joy Borum is a mediator in Scottsdale, Arizona. She took my first Soul Vows course in 2011. At the time, I taught soul vows only as a two-part covenant. I didn't know then that the path to soul vows was the chakras, and I had no awareness of the "new I."

When I asked Joy what it's been like living her soul vows for three years, she started laughing. "Let me give you one small example," she said. "A friend met me in a coffee shop recently with a gift she brought back from Argentina. It was on the table wrapped in brown paper. I said, 'I hope you won't be offended if I tell you what it is. It's a prayer shawl, isn't it?' She sputtered, 'Well, well, well . . . it might be.' Of course it was."

I asked Joy to talk about how she practices her soul vows. She has three:

God is all.

I trust and thank; I accept and share.

My work is our love.

Joy said her last vow was originally "My work is my love," but several months ago, she found herself spontaneously saying, "My work is *our* love." Now it was my turn to laugh, because without hearing anything about the "new I," Joy had intuited that our soul vows are so much more than a two-way covenant. So I told her about speaking her soul vows as "I, the Divine, . . . in Joy, through Joy, and as Joy," and "I, the one who . . . , is the one who is . . ." She was ecstatic and started playing with her vows immediately. When they disintegrated grammatically, Joy just laughed even more. "What a superb way to unjam the circuits!" She was so delighted with the "new I" that I told her about the sacred marriage, the chakras, and the swan, too.

Then I asked Joy how she incorporates her soul vows into her daily spiritual practice. Joy said she says the Prayer to Shamballa from the Agni Yoga Society's book *Agni Yoga*:

> O Thou, who called me to the path of labor
> Accept my ableness and my desire
> Accept my labor O Lord.
> Because by day and by night,
> Thou beholdest me,
> Manifest Thy hand O Lord.
> Because great is darkness,
> I follow Thee.

Then she intones *Om* and asks a question she finds in *An Inside Job* by Richard Reiger. She says this question silently three times and then aloud once: "Dearly Beloved Indwelling Holy Spirit, what is the first step toward Thy/my goal you want me to take beginning today?"

As she speaks the question aloud, Joy picks up a pen, because she knows she will receive an immediate response and wants to capture it. Joy has a unique deep-soul-writing method. She holds two different colored pens, one in each hand, and alternates writing what she is saying in her dominant hand and what Spirit is saying in her nondominant hand, back and forth, color by color.

"Since I've been living my soul vows," she said, "before I can even get my nondominant hand in motion, I *know* the answer I will be given. This morning, for example, I heard the word *run*. I thought, 'What?' and heard 'Look it up.' So I did, and *run* has pages of meanings. But there was one I knew was meant for me: 'to run strongly as the stream or the sea.' That was what I needed to hear."

I could see how Joy's soul vows were a rich part of her spiritual life, but I wondered if they helped her in her professional work as well.

"Oh yes!" she laughed, "I mediate with people who are *very* upset. During a meeting, I *am* aware of what is going on inside them. I keep it to myself, but sometimes it slips out. I often tell stories to try to normalize things people are struggling with. One day I used a story about a dentist racing bicycles, and the man looked at me in shock, '*How* did you *know* that?' I said I didn't know it. But on another level, of course, I did."

Joy ended our conversation with, "My soul vows are absolutely why I'm here this time. I know they are the core of my being, and I know they are leading me in everything I do." As Joy spoke of how fully she trusts her guidance, I felt I could see her swan flying back and forth between worlds carrying wisdom and grace, light and knowing.

Usha

Usha Sharma in Morgan Hill, California, had been living her soul vows for one year when I spoke with her. You met Usha when she shared the story of her bilingual *punya* vow and when she described her spiritual practices and her intimate party-of-two celebration. Usha's soul vows are:

> I lead with the Love I am.
>
> I am One.
>
> Shine the healing light of truth.
>
> Honor myself.
>
> Do *punya* with presence.

Pray in the present.

Unite and cocreate for truth, beauty, and good.

Surrender: God's way is here in every moment.

I am free.

Usha is a life coach—a divine life coach—to be precise. I asked Usha what it's been like to live her soul vows for one year. The first thing she mentioned was the connection between surrender and what she calls "the eye of knowing."

"One of my vows is to honor myself," she told me. "For me, honoring myself is honoring my body wisdom, trusting it. For example, one of the gifts I received through the process of finding my soul vow was the awareness that I am a healer. As a life coach, I have many tools in my kit and much training from wise mentors I adore, but I had never owned healing as one of my gifts or roles. But I surrender to my soul vows to be of service to others, so I had the thought to begin exploring healing.

"I was in my neighborhood Barnes & Noble, and noticed a book by Jose Silva. I'd never heard of Jose Silva. I picked it up and as I was walking over to sit down and look at it, I felt a bolt of energy shoot up my spine. I knew my energy wants me to love this book! I started reading it—and it's a book about healing!"

Usha went home to research Jose Silva online. She found dozens of his books, but her body wisdom directed her to buy one particular used copy of his autobiography. When it arrived, she saw that Jose Silva himself had inscribed it:

May God guide you to become attuned to the correct concepts of these experiences so that you may also help to make this planet a better world to live in.
Yours in the service to humanity,
Jose Silva

Usha said, "This was just so amazing. My soul vows are about expressing authentic power in service to all. I feel so connected. This is about honoring the energy when it rises in me, surrendering to that, listening, and taking the next step. I've led a spiritual group for women in Morgan Hill for four years. Two months ago, around the time of the experience with Jose Silva, everyone started bringing prayers they need for healing, and the entire healing experience has deepened our group to a whole new level."

I asked Usha to talk about how her soul vows support her coaching practice. She said, "What I've noticed is that one of my vows is about surrendering, and in my coaching, before I sit down to take a call, I stand in front of my altar, light a candle, and chant my vows. I ask, 'What is this person ready to heal right now, and help me be of service for that.' Then I sit down with my client. I've noticed that when I do this, my intuition is active throughout the call.

"Recently, for example, I mentioned the Prayer of St. Francis to a client. She was so surprised because she had just been looking at that prayer the night before. I had no intention of speaking about St. Francis or mentioning that prayer, but I felt that is how I was meant to be of service. This knowing is growing, and when I surrender to it, and trust it, I can be of greater service."

Wendy Kennedy

Wendy in Raleigh, North Carolina, coined the phrase I now consider a theme song for soul vows: "Before Soul Vows, Wendy 1.0; After Soul Vows, Wendy 2.0." But when you hear her story, I think you'll agree with me that she's becoming something more like Wendy 9.0.

Wendy came to the very first Soul Vows class in 2011. At the time, she said she wanted to answer her number one burning question, "Who is my authentic self?" and she felt soul vows would be an integral part of the answer. Here are Wendy's vows:

Breathe Deeply.
Live in the Now.

Walk in Joy and Happiness Daily.

Love Unconditionally.

I asked Wendy what it was like to "walk" her soul vows on her stairs (see the "Fifth Exploration" chapter). She laughed and said, "It makes me ridiculously happy and joyful, especially when I walk them at night. I call all my parts to be here now, then with joy I walk slowly, stopping at each one. I don't just say them, I *am* them. So when I say 'I breathe deeply,' I take a deep breath. As I say my last vow, 'I love unconditionally,' I kiss my puppy waiting for me at the top of the stairs."

Then I asked Wendy what it's like to live her soul vows. With glee, she said, "I continuously live in this experience of expansion and joy. I invoke divine order in my day every day, and then I say, 'OK heaven, let's go!' And no matter what happens, I trust my intuition. I know when people are lying. I just know. I know when things are going to happen long before they happen, and then when they happen, I don't get upset. I just look at what's happening and say 'Oh that's interesting! What's next?'"

Knowing how important authenticity is to Wendy, I asked if her perception and awareness of her self has changed. She laughed again.

"If you are really going to take this in, you cannot help but evolve, because you are bringing yourself closer and closer to your true authentic self, which is divinity," she said. "You realize there is no separation between you and anyone or anything else. All you can do is walk in kindness and love, do the things that Krishna, Jesus, Buddha, and Muhammad all asked us to do—be who you were made to be. You must embrace the mystic that you are."

Maggie

Maggie Reyes and her husband, Mariano, joined me on a soul journey to sacred Blackfeet land in Montana in 2012. Before each day's adventure, we chanted this little prayer I received at St. Michael's shrine the day before we left: *I am here. I am present. I am open. I am ready.*

Maggie and Mariano loved this prayer. They spoke it for us every day in Spanish. Both of them were fully present, and both had mystical experiences during our soul journey. Mariano came back one morning from a predawn walk with news that the elk herd he visited every morning had blessed him with a new name, "He Who Sees Beyond the Hills." Maggie said our little four-line prayer was invoking these powerful experiences because it ends with "I am ready."

"That's the prayer that generated my fabulous new job," she said, "and it's all because of my soul vows." That got my attention! I asked Maggie *how* her soul vows generated a great job.

She said, "Two years ago I was obsessed with the idea that if I had a mission and vision, everything would change, but all the books I found were too corporate. Then I found the Soul Vows course on your website and knew it was exactly what my soul was hungry for.

"One night during class, I suddenly I had to grab my laptop. My vows came in one moment:

I live in peace and joy.
I trust God's divine plan.
I see the good in everything.
I bless and I am blessed.
I feel complete.
I know what I need to know.
I am who I need to be.
I hear the Voice of my Soul.
I do what is mine to do.
All is well.

"At the beginning, every time I said my vows, it felt like opening a door. At the time, I was working in a job that was okay, but I felt my soul needing to grow. When I said, 'I see the good in everything,' it was a challenge. I'd get to work, and I'd think, 'How am I going to see the good in *this*?' And 'I feel complete' was huge. My whole life I struggled with not feeling good enough or feeling something was missing, so it was very powerful for me to say, 'I feel complete.'

"I kept saying and living my soul vows every day. Then I went to a workshop I thought was going to be about my purpose, but it turned out to be about how to create a soul-based business. That sparked my imagination in a way it had never been sparked before. I decided I wanted to be a life coach helping people be happily married. One day I wrote in my journal, 'I want to work with A players.' I said to myself, 'I don't know if I'll become a life coach in three months or three years, but I need to get ready.' So I went to work with a smile on my face and 'did what was mine to do,' and I starting clearing and cleaning so I could be ready.

"Good thing, too, because when it happened, it happened so fast! A recruiter called. I thought, 'If I weren't thinking of starting my own business, this would be my dream job.' Then it dawned on me, *this* is what's in front of me right now! *This* is what's mine to do! In my third interview with a super bigwig, he said, 'If you come to work here, you are going to be sur- rounded by A players.' He had no idea he was quoting me back to me!

"Now I have this dream job, and I'm a life coach, and I'm blogging at modernmarried.com, which has been recom- mended by the leading marriage researchers the Gottman Institute, and I've been invited to do live radio segments on DayBreak USA. I know I would not have been mentally or spiri- tually ready if I had not laid the groundwork with my soul vows. Everything goes back to my soul vows. My soul vows got me to a place where I could say 'I am ready.' My job now is simply to bless the world and be blessed in return, no matter what I'm doing. What a soul vow!"

I concur. "I bless and I am blessed" does summarize the essence of our soul vows. No matter who we are, or where we are, or what our particular soul vows are, in the end, as we gather the Presence of the Divine in and through and as us, we bless the world. And we are so blessed in return.

And I totally agree with Usha's summary: "This knowing is growing, and when I surrender to it, and trust it, I can be of greater service." The knowing *is* growing, but interestingly, the knowing is not the end; it is not the reason we live our soul vows. The true end, the divine purpose, is the call to surrender and put our knowing into service to others—just like Buckminster Fuller.

And I affirm with Joy, "My soul vows are absolutely why I'm here this time. I know they are the core of my being, and I know they are leading me in everything I do." And with Wendy, I bow to the profound truth, "All you can do is walk in kindness and love, do the things that Krishna, Jesus, Buddha, and Muhammad all asked us to do—be who you were made to be. You must embrace the mystic that you are."

These stories capture the divine dance of grace as we live our soul vows. And did you notice, it's a dance that leaves the dancers breathless with laughter and joy?

Trust the Dance

What keeps us from reaching that state of continuous expansion and joy? What stands in the way of experiencing that place of no separation? What holds us back from piercing the veils of time on the wings of the swan? What gets in the way of experiencing ourselves filled with light? What stops us from living life with gales of laughter? What keeps us from knowing—and knowing that what we know is true? Or as Wendy put it, what prevents us from being the mystics we were made to be?

I think the answer is simple. It's trust. Before the knowing comes trust in the knowing. Before piercing time comes trust that it can be pierced. Before the miracle comes trust in the miracle. You can hear that trust flowing through Joy's and Usha's and Maggie's and Wendy's stories and all the stories in this book. But trust is evident not only in people who have been living their soul vows for a few years; you can see it in yourself, too. You are here in the sixth chakra, stretching your swan wings and beginning your lifelong dance with your soul vows because you have walked in trust.

You walked in trust when you picked up this book. You walked in trust when you embraced your dual divine-human lineage in the first chakra, whether you understood it or not. You walked in trust when you called your critical voices forward and listened to their stories, trusting good would come of getting to know your false masters. In the third chakra, you walked in total trust when you released your false masters in a sacred ceremony of your own design, trusting your story together was complete. In the fourth chakra, you experienced your greatest trust walk of all—you stepped out of your logical, well-trained conscious mind and trusted your holy heart to hand you your soul vows. And it did. You trusted that these few precious divine qualities belong to you, even though you didn't really know what they mean. Then, in the fifth chakra, you trusted your vows to teach you their song. And they did. You took that song and began to sing it, trusting your soul vows prayer would sing you into being. And it has, and it is, and it will.

Now, in the sixth chakra, it all comes together as you trust your soul vows to gather the Presence of the Divine in you, through you, and as you, as you embody these precious values and pour their grace into the world. Perhaps you didn't realize it until just now, but you are becoming quite the master of trust.

Trust is important, because right about now you're probably wondering what will happen as you live your soul vows. Will everything be pretty and safe from this moment on? In a way, yes, but in a word, no. It's that paradox thing again. Your soul vows are not castle walls that keep out the hordes of loss. Despite the proclamations of hundreds of self-help programs, there actually are no such walls. In a videotaped conversation, David Whyte said in a matter-of-fact tone, "There is no competency that can protect you from life's losses." I stopped the video and played that line again. And again. And again. I spoke it aloud: "There *is* no competency that can protect you from life's losses." I sensed this was an essential truth, and I wanted to memorize it by heart.

Now, many people might hear this and be terrified. "What! There's nothing I can do to keep pain away? But I'm working so hard to do just that!" But I find this fact comforting at the deepest level. If there really is nothing I can do—no career I can build, no title I can hold, no degree I can earn, no amount of money I can save, no perfect relationship I can find, no perfect body I can build. If there really is nothing I can do to prevent the natural erosions that come with time and life, then, hooray, I can relax! Instead of striving ceaselessly to build hopelessly porous fortifications, I can simply open the door and welcome life in with open arms, saying, "Come dance with me! Come dance!"

Why? Because I can trust that this dance with life is a dance of divine *guide-dance.* God is the *guide,* and together, we are the *dance.* Even when the dance gets a bit wild, as it often does; or I can't quite hear the music, which happens sometimes; or the lights get low, and I can't see where we're headed on this tilted dance floor, I can still trust the dance. I can't see the whole picture, it's true, but I do know my seven little steps:

Step one: No matter what's happening, I continue to unite with people to create good in this world. And I always find them—or rather, they always find me. Together, we do something that matters, something that helps, something that heals. Coming together with 100 people to send light to the prison was a beautiful expression of this soul vow. This is my job description, and it's a great one. In fact, I think it calls for a little hop and skip step right now.

Step two: I treat everyone as a partner. We're all in this dance together. Someone at the counter in the airport may be my partner for five minutes, someone else for five years, a precious few for life, but with this soul vow I know we are all partners. In fact, I have so many partners that I think this step looks like Dances of Universal Peace with all of us, hundreds really, moving in gentle circles bending together to the music of the soul. Aaah, what a sweet dance move this one is.

Step three: I honor the Self in me. And because I honor the Self in me, I honor the Self in you, and the Self in her, and the Self in him, and the Self in them, and the Self in the grasses and the flowers and the trees. I can feel this soul vow in my body. It is a bow—a quiet slow and holy bow.

Step four: I never forget that I come from love and love is a balm to be shared. It's not mine to horde; it's mine to spread. And oh how it spreads, even over my enemies. The federal judge who put my Jerry in prison taught me that. I know that I come from love and I will return to love, and in the meantime I get to spread love. This step feels like a waltz glide.

Step five: I surrender! This is my starting point and my ending point. I always surrender because—surprise!—there actually is no path but God's. I am on that path. You are on that path. We are all on that path. There is no other path. I love this step. Surrender feels like a divine tango to me. And to think I fought the word *surrender* for years. Now surrender is my most holy companion.

Step six: I keep seeking Truth, and I know Truth keeps seeking me. Truth and I are friends. She dances me to places I'd never find on my own. So perhaps this is a jazz move with no planned choreography, just the intoxicating call of a saxophone in the distance. I follow where Truth beckons.

Step seven: My last dance step is a gentle sway. I pray. I'm praying right now as I write this, and I know you're praying right now as you read it. My life is a swaying prayer.

I love my seven little dance moves. When I dance the dance of my soul vows, I can trust that Presence is moving in me and through me into the world. When I twirl, I can trust that light is spinning off me to bless someone, even if I never know who or where or how. When I know, I can trust that I know, and I can follow intuition where she leads. When I dance the steps that are mine to dance, life can walk in the door with one of her crazy surprises or strange gifts, and I can dance in response.

Oh, and laugh. I mustn't forget laughter. That's what Hafiz recommends—and I'm certain Joy and Wendy and Usha and Maggie would gleefully agree.

> Tell me, love, what I need right now so that
> I might sing, and be alive, as my every cell
> craves.
>
> Tell me, dear, what I need right now, but
> in a manner I won't soon forget.
>
> Then the world began to sway, its hips
> invited my arms, its feet placed mine upon
> them, that made all my effort easy.
>
> A father's toes lifting a child's in dance caused
> God to pull out a drum.
>
> The Beloved belted out a tune, that went,
> "Nothing to follow . . . for I will move you.
> You need not do a damn thing . . . just laugh."
>
> Hafiz, "In a Manner I Won't Forget," from *A Year with Hafiz,*
> translation by Daniel Ladinsky

So now all you have to do is learn your dance moves. What are they? If it would be helpful—and fun—draw dance steps in your journal for each of your soul vows and ask your divine partner to teach you the moves. Then learn them—learn them so well, you know them by heart.

For a while, until your soul vows are fully embedded in your body and your consciousness, you might have to pause for a moment and think about how to live your soul vows. Life will be happy to help you with this. It will toss up the kinds of situations that were once guaranteed to trigger your false, unconscious responses. But you are no longer ruled by those masters, so now when something potentially upsetting happens, you have the luxury of an empty space in which to notice what's happening and *choose* how you want to respond. Step into that space. Take a moment and look at where you are. Take the situation into your cave of solitude and onto the page in deep soul writing and into prayer. Ask your divine Self questions like these:

> *Is this an opportunity to shine the light of my soul vows?*
>
> *How would my false masters have directed me to act in the past?*
>
> *What would it look like if I responded from my soul vows?*
>
> *How do I choose to respond to this situation?*

After a while, filtering all your decisions and relationships and choices through your soul vows will become automatic. You won't have to stop and slip into your cave of solitude. You won't even have to think about it. The day will come when you realize you *are your soul vows* and your soul vows *are you.*

Be the Light

Do you remember my little verbal slip when I got up to pray for my son and I blurted out, "It's time to *be* the prayer"? Well, in the sixth chakra, you get to "*Be* the light." You get to dance your share of the light into every corner of your world.

Your soul vows are not meant to stay in your cave of solitude or on your meditation cushion or prayer rug. Your soul vows came initially as a divine gift *to* you, but now you see that they are a divine gift that flows into the world *through* you. This is how you serve. But how do you keep this gift alive? How do you keep the flow flowing? How can you keep gathering the Presence in you, through you, and as you? How can you keep your soul vows so fresh and alive that you become the light? Here are a few thoughts. As you explore them, I know you will come up with more of your own.

Keep your spiritual practices alive. Engage in prayer and practice in some way every day. This is how you attune yourself to the light.

Chant or speak your soul vows with your whole being at least once a day. Your vows have so many surprises to share with you, but first you must become the best of friends.

Read mystical poetry—and read it out loud. On *The Soul-Directed Life,* Daniel Ladinsky explained, "No matter how you're feeling, read the poems out loud. It always plugs you in to a little higher level, where you want to be." When I'm bewildered, I turn to Hafiz. And he always—always—hands me the perfect words to soothe my aching heart.

Continue to spend time with your master-teacher companion. And when you've completed that one, ask to be led to another and another. There are so many magnificent teachers waiting for you to sit down beside them and listen as they tell you the great truths. And please don't settle for a feeble imitation. If your intuition tells you someone or something is not fully attuned to the light, put the book down or gently walk away. Fill your spiritual library with light, so that when you walk in the room or pick up your e-reader or listen to recordings, you glow.

Keep playing with paradox. Wrestle with it. Squeeze out all the startling new knowings you can. The more you play with paradox, the closer you get to God. I really do think it's that simple.

Pay attention. The light is in conversation with you every moment of every day. You just have to notice. Remember, the soul takes nothing for granted.

Locate your intuition and knowing. Buckminster Fuller *heard* his knowing. Usha Sharma *feels* her "body wisdom." I *saw* the covers of my books. But you may perceive intuition and knowing in other ways. Review the clairs—clairaudience, clairvoyance, clairsentience, and claircognizance—and pay attention to which ones are trying to get your attention. Everyone has the potential for all four, but usually one or two are most active. Notice where and how your soul delivers knowing—then follow.

Get to know your mystical messengers. When my first teacher, Charlotte Starfire, opened my eyes to the medicine of the animals in the tradition of the First People, every animal on my path became a teacher. A lizard was a reminder to pay attention to my dreams. A snake shedding its skin on my doorstep was a harbinger of transmutation. The grasshopper tapping at my glass door one summer day delivered news of a major leap that did indeed come five months later. Without this sensitivity to the messages of the animals, the swan might have flown right past me. A few years ago, Margo Mastromarchi came into my life and taught me about angels. Now I perceive loving guidance and support everywhere and always. Even my dreams are full of news from my soul's playground. You, too, are surrounded by messengers; who are they?

Do what is yours to do. I'm borrowing one of Maggie's vows here. How will you know what is yours to do? In your ever-expanding state of clear knowing, you will sense it. You will. The key is to do it.

Stay in love with the sacred marriage. The oddest thing happens when you do: you end up in love with *all of it*—all of life, all the people, all the experiences, all the trees, all the stars. Throughout Julian of Norwich's showings, she wondered why God was revealing all he was revealing to her. Her answer came fifteen years later in a spiritual vision: "Would you like to know our Lord's meaning in all this? Know it well: love was his meaning. Who revealed this to you? Love. What did he reveal? Love. Why did he reveal it to you? For love. Stay with this and you will know more of the same. You will never know anything but love, without end" (from *The Showings of Julian of Norwich*, translation by Mirabai Starr).

I find I can't hold this love in. I sing out "I love my house!" as I walk down the stairs in the morning and "I love my coffee!" at the first sip. I shout "I love my Jerry!" every time I see a text from him. When my radio show ends, I cry, "I love this show!" And when I read John O'Donohue or Kabir Helminski or Hafiz or any of my beloved companions, I pat the book and sigh, "I love you." I whisper "I love you" to my computer, my car, my mother's crystal, and my bank—yes, even my bank. You won't be able to contain yourself, either. The sacred marriage is inviting you into a love relationship with all of life. So go *be* the love! You know how to *be* the prayer and *be* the light; you're ready to go all the way and *be* the love!

Be grateful. Always, always, always be grateful to life, whether you understand it or not. As Rainer Maria Rilke said in his Ninth Elegy, "*Truly* being here is so much." He emphasized the word *truly*, and thanks to our soul vows, we are truly present, truly honoring the mystery, truly in the dance.

Sixth Paradox: I Know That I Know; I Know That I Don't Know

You and I will be in this sixth-chakra energy for a long time. I think it's going to take a lifetime to explore the many ways we embody the Presence of the Divine and spread our share of the light as we live our soul vows. So don't feel rushed. You have plenty of time to play with all the paradoxes in the sixth chakra. And there are many, aren't there?

The first one I tripped over, the moment I entered the sixth chakra and discovered it was the chakra of knowing, is that knowing itself is a paradox. The more I know that I know—and I do experience claircognizance all the time—the more I can see that I don't have a clue *how* I know or *what* I know or *why* I know something. All I can do is receive the gift and put it to use. So knowing is a mystery to me. I have to stay in a state of trust with knowing because the truth is, I don't know how this works. Plus, the more I know, the more I can see that what I know is an infinitesimal speck of all there is to be known. For example:

How was the universe formed? I don't know.

Why was the universe formed? I don't know.

What is the Divine? I surely don't know.

What is the meaning of life? We've been asking this question for millennia, and we still don't know.

Why do bad things happen? Wish I knew the answer to this one.

What is evil and where does it come from? I don't know.

How many times have I been here?

Have I been other than human?

What will happen when I shed this form?

What exactly is forgiveness?

What is a soul?

And so many other great philosophical and spiritual questions. For these, and hundreds more, all I can say is, I know that I don't know the answers. In fact, the more I do know, the more I know I don't know. That's the paradox I'm befriending in this sixth chakra of knowing.

My triangle says on the left "I know that I know" in celebration of the great gift of illuminated knowing. But then, on the opposite side, I wrote, "I know that I don't know," because that's the truth!

What arises out of this apparent conflict? "I trust." For me, the mystery of light and knowing in the sixth chakra is simply to trust the mystery—trust that I don't have and won't have all the answers, trust that my soul vows are carrying me where I need to go, trust that this is a divinely constructed universe,

and trust that my part in it matters. The perfect image to capture the beauty of the many mysteries in the sixth chakra is my
new best friend, the swan. I am happy to ride the swan for the
rest of my life.

What about you? What mysteries have you been wrestling
with in the sixth chakra? We've tumbled into so many. Buckminster Fuller's "You do not belong to you; you belong to the
universe" is a beautiful one. Have you asked yourself to whom
you belong? Or perhaps you're still trying to figure out how
the original meaning of "light shall be" in Hebrew is the same
as "light was." The union of all time in this time is a wonderful
conundrum, isn't it? The greatest minds in science are wrestling with that one, so you're in good company. How would
you write the paradox of time? Maybe something like "Now is
now; now is not now."

And then there's the entire point of this chakra exploration
and the mysterious truth expressed in the very first poem of this
book by Hafiz: each soul completes God. *That* is a true mystery of
creation. How would you say *that* on your triangle? "I complete
God" is a pretty astonishing statement.

There are so many delicious paradoxes in this chakra of light that you may want to make multiple triangles and revisit them for years to come.

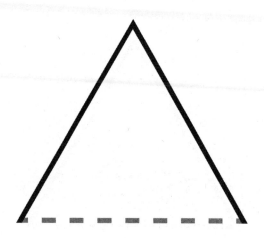

Sixth Discovery: I Trust

Just as there are endless paradoxes in the sixth chakra, I think there are many, many discoveries. When I first started this book, I thought the discovery for the sixth chakra would be "I gather," because that is what is happening at this stage in our relationship with our soul vows: we are gathering the Presence of the Divine in and through and even as us. It's still so miraculous; it takes my breath away just to type that sentence. And so I thought "I gather" would be a lovely discovery to put in our pockets till the end of our days.

But my own intuitive knowing kept growing as I wrote this chapter, and I felt a nonnegotiable pull to look *beneath* "I gather" to find an even deeper core discovery. When I did, I immediately found "I trust." Of course! Before the gathering, there is trust in the gathering. So the discovery I have put in my pocket is "I trust." And I know that trust in the Divine is really the only thing I need in my pocket ever.

What about you? What discoveries are you making in this sixth-chakra exploration of light and knowing and gathering? Is it "I gather," or "I trust," or perhaps "I dance with the mystery," or "I belong to the universe," or "I am the light"? There are so many divine discoveries here. Choose one or two or ten for that matter, and put them in your pocket. You don't have to understand them right now. They will reveal themselves to you over time. From within your pocket they will whisper to you to look and see and know and feel the truth that you are.

Seventh Exploration

live in sacred unity

Seventh Chakra: Crown Chakra
Seventh Paradox: There are no opposites.
Seventh Discovery: I am One.

The minute I heard my first love story,
I started looking for you, not knowing
how blind that was.

Lovers don't finally meet somewhere,
they're in each other all along.

From *The Essential Rumi*, translation by Coleman Barks

When I contemplated writing this exploration, I didn't know what I could say because I have little personal experience of mystical union with the Beloved. My Shakti-soul-self is still very busy and very happy playing in the vast fields of the sixth chakra with all its light and knowing and trust. Every day in that playground, there is a discovery, a joy, a twist, a kiss. I have still so much to learn and see and do in the sixth chakra.

And yet—and yet—I want to enter the seventh, too. I want to be one with the One. That's what I really meant when I cried, "I want You to find me. I will sit in a field until You find me!" Back then I saw myself alone in a field, waiting *to be* found; today

I see I've never been alone and I am *already* found. I see that. I know that. I even feel that. And yet I sense I haven't entered the seventh chakra. I am still reading about, learning about, talking about, studying about, and opening to the mystical truths at the center of life. I think that's why I've invited so many mystics and students of mysticism to talk with me on *The Soul-Directed Life*.

I am hungry for mystical union. And after all your adventures in *Soul Vows*, you are too. So I thought the best I could do for you—and for me—in this final chakra exploration would be to quote mystics from all traditions who left word of their own ecstatic unions. I went on a hunt for the most beautiful and eloquent prayers and poems and quotations I could find. And the funniest thing happened. I realized I actually did have much to share with you in this deep soul exploration of the seventh chakra.

Welcome to the crown chakra, at the top of your head, where so many miracles await. Here, Shakti will at last unite with her beloved Shiva, and you, too, will unite with all you have been longing for. Here, your sense of who you are will complete its transformation from self to Self, from two to One, from separation to Union. Here, your awareness of duality will dissolve, and as it does, you, too, will dissolve, like a grain of salt in the ocean of Love. And, like the mystics of the ages, you will begin to glow with joy.

Deep Soul Explorations

In this seventh deep soul exploration in the seventh chakra, you will:

- listen to the voices of the mystics
- write your own declaration
- unite Shakti and Shiva in bliss
- connect the first and seventh chakras and complete the circle of sacred unity
- become the glowing hologram that you are
- circle back to the beginning

Listen to the Voices of the Mystics

The words of the mystics can best prepare us for the experience of sacred union. Here are a few ecstatic messages across cultures and continents, in approximate chronological order, beginning with the Upanishads recorded in India in the sixth century BCE, the Torah written shortly thereafter in the Middle East, and the Tao Te Ching, believed to be written in the fourth century BCE in China, then moving through the centuries to the present. Read these words slowly, in your own style of *lectio divina,* and let their perfume reach your heart.

This tremendous equation—"the self is Braham"—is the central discovery of the Upanishads. Its most famous formulation is one of the mahavakyas or "great formulae": Tat tvam asi, "You are That." "That" is the characteristic way the Upanishads point to the Reality that cannot be described; and "you," of course, is not the petty, finite personality, but that pure consciousness "which makes the eye see and the mind think": the Self.

Introduction to *The Upanishads,* Eknath Easwaran

I am my beloved's, and my beloved is mine.

The Song of Solomon 6:3, *Holy Bible from the Ancient Eastern Text,* translation by George M. Lamsa

Create for me a pure heart.

[God] has created for me a pure heart.

O pure heart, create for me [the experience of] God.

The pure heart has created God for me.

Psalm 51:12, four Midrashic translations by Rabbi Shefa Gold, *The Magic of Hebrew Chant*

He who knows the play of Tao and Te

knows the nature of the universe

live in sacred unity   201

Tao brings forth Te from its own being
Te expands in all directions
filling every corner of the world
becoming the splendor of all creation
Yet at every moment Te seeks Tao
This is the movement that guides the universe
This is the impulse
that leads all things back home

Tao Te Ching, verse 65, translation by Jonathan Star

The Father and I are One. The Father is in me and I am in the Father.

Gospel of John 10:30, 38, *The New Jerusalem Bible*

The birds have vanished in the sky
and now the last cloud drains away.
We sit together, the mountain and me,
until only the mountain remains.

Li Po, eighth-century Chinese poet, translation by Sam Hamill

We awaken as the Beloved in every last part of our body.

Symeon the New Theologian, eleventh-century
Byzantine Eastern Orthodox monk, in *The Enlightened Heart:
An Anthology of Sacred Poetry*, edited by Stephen Mitchell

The sun of majesty sent forth his rays, and in the reflection of each other's faces these thirty birds (si-murgh) of the outer world, contemplated the face of the Simurgh of the inner world. This so astonished them that they did not know if they were still themselves or if they had become the Simurgh. At last, in a state of contemplation, they realized that they were the Simurgh and that the Simurgh was the thirty birds. When they gazed at the Simurgh they saw that it was truly the Simurgh who was there, and when they turned their eyes toward themselves they saw that they themselves were the Simurgh. And perceiving both at once, themselves and Him, they realized that they and the Simurgh were one and the same being. No one in the world has ever heard of anything to equal it.

Farid ud-Din Abu Attar, twelfth-century Persian Sufi poet,
The Conference of the Birds, translation by C. S. Nott
(*The Conference of the Birds* is considered one of the most
significant works of Persian literature and the precursor
to the great tradition of Sufi mystical poetry.)

There is no better statement of the first attribute [realizing the divinity of self] than this one written by the kabbalist Abraham Abulafia in the thirteenth century: "Behold you are God and God is you; for you are so intimately adhering to God that you cannot by any means be separate from God, for you are God. See now that I, even I, am God. He is I and I am He.

Abraham Abulafia, thirteenth-century Kabbalist,
in *The Sacred Art of Lovingkindness*, Rabbi Rami Shapiro

God being in himself pure good can dwell nowhere except in the pure soul. He overflows into her Whole, he flows into her . . . She is so clear she sees through herself; nor is God far to seek: she finds him in herself when in her natural purity she flows into the supernatural pure Godhead, here she is in God and God in her, and what she does, she does in God and God does it in her.

Meister Eckhart, fourteenth-century Dominican theologian,
*Meister Eckhart, from Whom God Hid Nothing:
Sermons, Writings, and Sayings*, edited by David O'Neal

I saw that there is no greater stature in this life than that of a child, who is naturally humble and free from the encumbrances of power and intelligence, until our Divine Mother brings us up to the bliss of our Divine Father.

Julian of Norwich, fourteenth-century English anchoress,
The Showings of Julian of Norwich, translation by Mirabai Starr

We

bloomed in Spring.

Our bodies

are the leaves of God.

The apparent seasons of life and death

our eyes can suffer;

but our souls, dear, I will just say this forthright:

they are God

Himself,

we will never perish

unless He

does.

St. Theresa of Avila, sixteenth-century Spanish Carmelite nun
and mystic, "I Will Just Say This," from *Love Poems from God*,
translation by Daniel Ladinsky

That mirror you (God) stand before—

we need to gaze into it also.

That name you called Beloved

as I fell from your lips—

I suffer

because I did not quite

hear it.

So tell me again dear One

so clear:

I am

you.

Tukaram, seventeenth-century Marathi poet, excerpt from
"How Could a Lover Fall?" from *Love Poems from God*,
translation by Daniel Ladinsky

[W]ithin man is the soul of the whole; the wise silence; the universal beauty, to which every part and particle is equally related, the eternal ONE. And this deep power in which we exist and whose beatitude is all accessible to us, is not only self-sufficing and perfect in every hour, but the act of seeing and the thing seen, the seer and the spectacle, the subject and the object, are one. WE see the world piece by piece, as the sun, the moon, the animal, the tree, but the whole, of which these are shining parts, is the soul.

Ralph Waldo Emerson, nineteenth-century
American transcendentalist, *Essays: First Series: 1*

Divine am I inside and out,

and I make holy whatever I touch or am touched from,

The scent of these arm-pits aroma finer than prayer,

This head more than churches, bibles, and all creeds.

Walt Whitman, nineteenth-century American poet
and humanist, *Song of Myself*

The great sea moves me, sets me adrift.

It moves me like algae on stones in running brook water.

The vault of heaven moves me

Mighty weather storms through my soul.

It carries me with it.

Trembling with joy.

Uvavnuk, twentieth-century Iglulik Inuit shamaness,
in *The Woman in the Shaman's Body*, Barbara Tedlock

Again and again I am conscious that I am seeking God. . . . With sustained excitement, I recall what, in my own urgency, I had forgotten: God is seeking me. Blessed remembrance! God is seeking me. Wonderful assurance. God is seeking me. This is the meaning of my longing, this is the warp of my desiring, this is my point. The searching that keeps the hot sand under my feet is but my response to His seeking. Therefore, this moment, I will be still, I will quiet my reaching out, I will abide; for to know really that God

live in sacred unity   205

is seeking me; to be aware of that now is to be found of Him. Then, as if by a miracle, He becomes the answer to my need. It sufficeth now and forever that I am found of Him.

Howard Thurman, twentieth-century American theologian and civil rights leader, *Meditations of the Heart*

The feeling of longing in your heart was not put there by yourself. We have seen how each of us was conceived in longing, and every moment here has been a pilgrimage of longing. Your life is a path of longing through ever-changing circles of belonging. Your longing echoes the Divine Longing. The heart of transcendence is longing.

John O'Donohue, contemporary poet, Celtic writer, and Catholic scholar, *Eternal Echoes*

God made humans so that humans can become God. A human being is a mini-God, a micro-theos who has been created in order to participate in the divinity of God. Deification is made not only of the spirit but of the body of a human, also.

Thich Nhat Hanh, contemporary Vietnamese Zen Buddhist monk and peace activist, *Living Buddha, Living Christ*

[F]or the Sufis the greatest secret of creation is that we are one with God. . . . Our Beloved whom we have longed for is in our heart in such intimacy that there are no longer two, but one. We are with our Beloved in complete oneness. This is when the love affair becomes fulfilled, a fulfillment that is tangible, that lives inside of us with every breath—it is intimate, it is oneness, and it is love.

Llewellyn Vaughan-Lee, contemporary Sufi mystic, *Fragments of a Love Story*

Mother of God
similar to fire,
ignite my heart in prayer.

Where once I stood on familiar ground,

selecting my spiritual experiences

like choice morsels from a well-tended larder,

now my garden has gone up in flames

and I thirst only for the Living God.

Let me find him, Mother,

as you do,

deep inside my own ripening being.

Let me swallow the Sacred

and burn with that Presence,

illuminating a way home to the Truth.

Lit from within,

let my blazing heart become a sanctuary

for the weary traveler,

until this long night lifts

and dawn unfolds her new radiance.

Mirabai Starr, contemporary leader of the interspirituality
movement, author, and translator of the mystics,
Mother of God Similar to Fire

Write Your Own Declaration

As you can hear in the river of words across time, the expressions of longing for divine union are unlimited. And yet, in the end, don't they all sound the same? They all speak of this flow, this movement, this melting of the individual soul into the One Soul. It's astonishing, but I think all this ecstasy can be condensed into one short line such as:

I am That.

I am my Beloved's and my Beloved is mine.

The Father and I are One.

I wrote my own one-line summation on a falcon wing on my 2013 Intention Mandala and now I say it several times a day: *I am one with the One.* This could be the sign on the door to my seventh chakra. What's on the door to yours? How would you summarize the profound mystical truth that has tantalized mystics of all time and is now beckoning you to enter your own chakra of union?

This is a perfect question to take into your cave of solitude for prayer, meditation, and deep soul writing. It's also a lovely question to hold in your heart as you sit with your master-teacher companion. A phrase, an image, a sentence, a word will pop off the page or come wafting on the wind. Listen for it. That's how I found all these quotes. I asked to be led to the perfect sources and my intuition—perhaps riding on the wings of the swan—led me where I needed to go. Sometimes I'd feel the urge to pick up an old friend and reread passages I had underlined. Sometimes I'd feel a pull to read something brand new to me. And sometimes, I'd feel a directive to pick up a book, like Llewellyn Vaughan-Lee's *Fragments of a Love Story*, hold it to my heart, and simply open it. Always, my eyes would land on something beautiful about our longing for the Beloved.

Ask your wise body with all its clairs to lead you to the words or images your heart wants to hear. Then ask your precious soul a few questions such as:

What quotes or poems describe my own longing for union with the Beloved?

Is there something else I feel called to read or do?

If I could distill my longing to a line or phrase and post it on the door to my crown chakra, what would it say?

Unite Shakti and Shiva in Bliss

This journey began in the first chakra, where you recognized Shakti's longing for Shiva as your own desire for union with the Divine. As your Shakti-soul-self moved through the adventures of the chakras, have you felt that desire expanding in energy and movement? Did reading the words of thousands of years of mystics excite your heart to finally, finally, want to be home? I spent three days reading nothing but the ecstatic words of the mystics in order to find the quotes you just read. By mid-afternoon each day, the top of my head would feel so cold, I'd have to stop and take a hot shower. I didn't understand what was happening until I opened *Chakras* by Harish Johari and read about the seventh chakra.

In that book's table of contents, all the chakras are listed in order, but between the sixth and the seventh there is an extra chapter on the *Soma* chakra. Soma does not have a number. Soma is a chakra *within* the energy of the seventh, but it is so important that it has its own name, special purpose, and unique location above your third eye. It is here in Soma that Shakti, the soul, is united with Shiva, the Beloved, the One, the Self. And in that union, the essence of the individual soul is absorbed into the essence of the One Soul. In this state of union in the Soma chakra, you experience bliss.

Bliss—isn't that a perfect word to describe what the mystics are trying to tell us? And bliss, I was stunned to read, is *cool*. No wonder I needed a hot shower. The cool bliss of the mystics' words kept jumping off the page and diving into my Soma chakra. This explains why we say "I got chills" when we read or hear something that our body recognizes as an otherworldly truth. Any experience of union, no matter how fleeting, is a moment of cool bliss.

This might be a good time to stop, look back at your own experiences, and honor all the times you have had moments of union, moments of cool bliss. I'll tell you one of mine. When it happened, I did not recognize it as a Soma experience, but now I see that it was.

In the summer of 2012, I took a small group to the Blacktail Ranch in Montana. One of the highlights of the trip was a private tour of an unaltered, ice-age cave on the property. There were no railings, ramps, or walkways inside. To get in, we slowly backed down a hand-hewn twenty-foot ladder, then crouched down and stumbled forward until we reached a large wet rock. We had to get down on our bums and slide into the cave. But once we could stand up and look around, we realized we were in the womb of mother earth and ancient brethren had been here before us. They left petroglyphs on the walls and an altar stone with a bison carved on one side and a bear on the other. They cooked here, they slept here, they worshipped here. We were in holy ground.

We asked our guide to leave us alone in the dark for ten minutes. He left and turned off the gas generator that powers the few lights. It didn't matter if my eyes were open or closed, but I still closed them; it felt more reverent. The cave was not silent. There were puffs of cold air and a chorus of mysterious drips. I swear I heard a few stones groan. The rocks emitted a perfume that cannot be described. In the silence, I asked the massive stone ceiling above me, "Do you have a message for me?"

The stones delivered a message that arrived inside of me. No seeing, hearing, or feeling was involved. It was an automatic transmission or infusion. The voice of the stones was simply inside me, and the rock said, "I am old. You are old." At first, I thought, "Uh no, rock, it's *you* who are old—ice-age old, glacial rivers carved you. I, on the other hand, am just sixty-four." But I wasn't about to argue with the bones of the earth. So I was still and allowed the rocks to repeat inside of me over and over, "I am old. You are old."

After a few minutes, I realized the pronouns had shifted, and I had begun telling the rocks, "I am old. You are old." That's the moment the wisdom I now recognize as Soma-chakra wisdom burst open inside me. I sensed the rocks were smiling as they watched me awaken to the truth: I am a soul, and souls are old—so old we call them "immortal." But if a soul is immortal, it is not just old; it is old-old—older than the rocks old. I was stunned by the depth of this knowing. This was the first time I knew—and knew that I knew—that I was a soul, and as a soul I was in touch with, and a part of, all that is, all that was, and all that will be, including these eloquent ancient stones.

Have you had an experience like that? A moment of knowing that you are connected with mother earth or father sky? Then you've had a taste of blissful union in the Soma chakra. And if you haven't (or think you haven't), then today's the day. Step outside in nature. Sit beneath a tree, on a rock, or beside the water. If that's not an option, step into your cave of solitude, breathe slowly, and imagine yourself in a redwood forest, or an ice-age cave, or above a gorge, or beside the ocean. Ask the trees or the stones or the water, "Do you have a message for me?" Then simply be still, and allow the tree or the rock or the ocean to speak to you.

Notice if, at some point, the gap between you and the "thing" you are communing with disappears. Notice how the two of you merge. In the end, there is no rock, no tree, no ocean; there is only a dissolving of the two into the One, and a sensation of cool bliss.

Remember the boy in the Upanishads who learned from the swan? Later in that same Chandogya Upanishad, we are introduced to another young boy, Shvetaketu. His father had sent Shvetaketu as a young boy to study with a great teacher. When he returned twelve years later, his father asked if he had learned to hear the unheard, or think the unthought, or know the unknown. The boy said, "No, Father, please teach me." His father proceeds to give Shvetaketu many lessons on the Self through natural things like nectar and trees and seeds.

One day, the father tells the boy to put some salt in water. The father asks, "Where is the salt?" And the boy says, "I do not see it." So the father tells him to sip the water and, of course, it is salty; it is salty everywhere. The father says:

"It is everywhere, though we see it not.
Just so, dear one, the Self is everywhere,
Within all things, although we see him not.
There is nothing that does not come from him.
Of everything he is the inmost Self.
He is the truth; he is the Self supreme.
You are that, Shvetaketu; you are that."

The Upanishads, translation by Eknath Easwaran

When the walls between you and the rocks, or you and the salt, or you and anything, melt, you too can say "I am that." For an advanced mystic, this state might be permanent; for you and me, it might last no longer than a moment, a whisper, a glance, a sigh. Even if it disappears as quickly as it came, it still came. And it's real. And for the moment, that is bliss enough.

Connect the First and Seventh Chakras and Complete the Circle of Sacred Unity

Here we are in the seventh chakra, at what appears to be the terminus of our journey. It's not an accident that the last chakra is the seventh. Seven is a mystical number. The seventh heaven is the highest heaven in the cosmology of many religions. This idea is so universal that we say "I'm in seventh heaven" without realizing we are affirming a mystical view of the universe.

Think back to the beginning of this adventure. Before we set foot in the first chakra, I shared Cynthia Bourgeault's declaration that *all* developing processes go through seven distinct phases. And we have certainly done that. We have traveled through seven very different spiritual adventures, all building one upon the other, and along the way we met and fell in love with our soul vows. We've even had a taste of bliss. But we're not finished. The chakras have a few more mystical surprises for us.

The seventh chakra is often depicted as a thousand-petaled lotus pointing downward, like a tight cap covering the top of the head. The crown chakra is the seat of the Self, the void that is all, the One, the Mystery. This is where the soul reaches perfection, Christ consciousness, enlightenment—any of the words humanity uses to try to name the unnamable state of sacred union. The path to this divine crown looks like a ladder. Images of the chakras invariably show them in a straight line starting at the base of the spine and climbing to the top of the head.

That is the image I held throughout this journey. I drew the chakra numbers one through seven on my whiteboard in a straight vertical line and next to each drew the image that captured the essence of that chakra for me and its discovery. The chakra ladder on my whiteboard looked like this:

7   I am one

6   I trust

5   I surrender

4   I am open

3   I am whole

2   I am free

1   I am ready

When I was halfway through writing this chapter, I was awakened one morning with the whiteboard image in my head. I often hear guidance, but I only rarely see it, so I knew this image was special. I kept still, waiting for something to happen—and it did. The first chakra began to move outward, away from the line and slowly curve up toward the seventh. When they met, they formed a perfect circle.

I burst out laughing. Of course! Why didn't I see this before? In the first chakra, we acknowledge our dual lineage; we embrace the truth, "I am human; I am divine." And what's the truth of the seventh? "I am one with the One." The seventh is the completion of the spark of knowing in the first. The sacred heart of the first becomes sacred unity in the seventh. We haven't been climbing a ladder at all! We've been walking a sacred spiral, a labyrinth, a circle, and now we are home where we started in our glorious embodied soul.

I am so grateful for this sweet image. It washes away any judgment of how we are "progressing" on the path. The path is a circle, and it will always carry us to sacred unity with the Beloved. It has to—a circle has no beginning and no end. The Celts knew this. John O'Donohue reminds us in book after book that the Celts saw all of life as a circle. The Native Americans knew this. The saint of the Oglala Sioux Black Elk said, "You have noticed

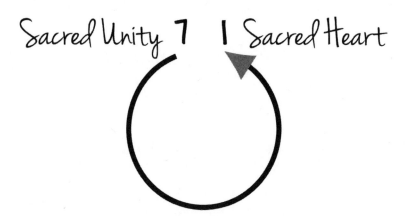

soul vows

that everything an Indian does is in a circle, and that is because the Power of the World always works in circles, and everything tries to be round" (*Black Elk Speaks*). And now we know this. Our personal sacred heart is, and was, and always will be one in sacred unity. We have arrived where we started, and we are home.

Become the Glowing Hologram That You Are

What does a soul look like when it rounds the circle and unites with the Beloved? What do *you* look like as you gather more and more of the Presence of the Divine in you, through you, and as you as you embody your soul vows? Have you asked yourself that question?

When Satyakama, the herd-tending boy in the Upanishads, returned to his master filled with the wisdom he learned about the Self from the bull, the fire, the swan, and the diving bird, his master called out, "You glow like one who has known the truth." I think the master was seeing Satyakama's halo. For eons, artists have placed halos around the head of gods, goddesses, Buddha, Jesus, angels, saints, and perfected ones. The halo is the universal symbol of the light of the Divine. So do you have a halo?

Harish Johari tells us that in the crown chakra "[t]he yogi becomes illuminated like the sun, a bright being, an enlightened master. His or her aura is continually radiant." Perhaps you and I are not exactly enlightened masters, but through our soul vows, we *are* gathering divine Presence and planting it in real, tangible, touchable, seeable ways on earth. So I daresay we can all put little halos around our heads, perhaps just a thin gold wire, and then, as we embody our divine qualities, that little line of light will grow. If the first-chakra discovery that we are both human and divine is true, then we've always had little gold halos; we just didn't know it. Now we do.

If you have a wisp of a halo now, what do you think will happen as you gather more and more of the divine Presence through your soul vows and shine more and more divine light into the world? To answer that question, I went to two sources that at first appear to be very different: the ancient Vedic tradition and modern quantum science. First from *Chakras*, by Harish Johari:

> Sahasrara [the seventh chakra] is the seat of the self-luminous soul or *chitta*, the essence of being. In the person who has attained Sahasrara, *chitta* is like a screen upon which the reflection of the cosmic Self, the divine, is seen. In the presence of the cosmic Self, it is possible for anyone to feel the divine and, indeed, to realize the divinity within oneself.

I reread this passage several times. I knew it was telling me something important, but I couldn't quite grasp it. So I set *Chakras* aside for a moment and thought I'd take a look at Larry Dossey's new book *One Mind*. Larry Dossey is a master at explaining the intersection of science and spirituality in language a nonscientist can understand. In his opening chapter, I stumbled upon this quote by Erwin Schrödinger, who won the Nobel Prize in 1933 for the discovery of wave mechanics:

> [As] inconceivable as it seems to ordinary reason, you—and all other conscious beings as such—are all in all. Hence this life of yours which you are living is not merely a piece of the entire existence, but is in a certain sense the *whole*; only this whole is not so constituted that it can be surveyed in one glance. This, as we know, is what the Brahmins express in that sacred mystic formula: Tat tvam asi, this is you. Or again, in such words as "I am in the east and in the west, I am below and above, *I am this whole world*."

What is something when it's not a piece of the whole, but the whole itself? A hologram. All the information of a hologram is present in any part of the hologram. So that ancient "screen upon which the reflection of the cosmic Self is seen" is the hologram Schrödinger describes twenty-seven hundred years later.

And that jewel image of our individual souls expressing one facet of the divine, why, it's a hologram! And your personal soul vows, why, they're a hologram of the depth and breadth of the qualities of the Divine.

It is a never-ceasing amazement that the ancients knew the truth so long ago: I am That. You are That. We are That. We are holograms of the Divine. Yes, indeed, the first chakra had it right all along. And we have come full circle from a sense of our small self, with roots to the earth, to an awareness of divine Self, which is the root of all there is. Like the boy in the Upanishads, we are returning from our deep soul explorations all aglow with the radiant light of the Divine.

Seventh Paradox: There Is No Paradox

In all our previous explorations, the paradox at the heart of the chakra jumped to the forefront pretty quickly. We could hardly miss it. We started wrestling with that paradox practically the moment we opened the door. But everything is different here in the seventh. Once Shakti merged with Shiva, once we realized we'd circled round to where we began, once our individual sacred heart melted into sacred unity, once we saw that our one self is a hologram of the total Self, we stopped being able to even see opposites. Shakti is now Shiva; Shiva is Shakti. The first chakra is the seventh; the seventh is the first. Our neighbor is us; we are our neighbor. Heaven is in earth; earth is in heaven. The beginning is the end; the end is the beginning. Salt can't be separated from water. You can't be separated from God. Your facet of the jewel is the Jewel. There is one hologram, one unity—Sacred Unity. Duality has dissolved. Paradox has disappeared. So I don't have a paradox triangle for you. The triangle itself has morphed into a circle.

Let me show you the circle I've drawn for my seventh-chakra adventure into sacred unity. The circle is the first shape in sacred geometry. It represents wholeness, completion, unity. Inside my circle I'm adding two crossed lines. Those lines represent several things for me. I followed the shape of the quartered circle when I said the Perfect Prayer over my son's bowl of freedom for the 253 days he was in prison. Plus, Jerry announced when he was just nine that the quartered circle was his symbol, and I had it painted on his curtains and bedspread and even took him to a blacksmith to have one made out of iron. And now when I say my soul vows, I often move my hands in a downward line for "in Janet," a crossed line for "through Janet," and a big circle for "as Janet."

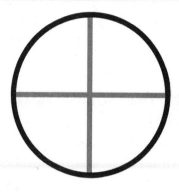

What circular shape would you like to draw for your own end-of-paradox adventure in the seventh chakra? A labyrinth? A spiral? The traditional thousand-petaled lotus? How about a hand mudra signifying wholeness? Or a mandala? Or a tantric symbol? Draw a symbol that represents cosmic unity for you.

Seventh Discovery: I Am One

What is the great discovery in this majestic crown chakra? "I am That. You are That." Or perhaps "I am the whole. You are the whole. We are the whole." For two years now I have been saying, "I am one with the One"; that could also be, "The One is me and I am in the One" or the new awareness "I am a hologram of the Divine."

I find myself wanting to shorten my summation to simply, "I am One." If I am the prayer and I am the love and I am the light, then perhaps I can say, "I am One."

Hafiz, too, searched for how to speak this great discovery:

> Inseparate is any creature or object from Light,
> from the Ocean, became my discovery.

> excerpt from "I Wade Out Into Other Forms," from *A Year With Hafiz*,
> translation by Daniel Ladinsky

How will you capture the mystical truth at the center of this soul vows adventure? Write it down and put it in your pocket.

You now have a pocket full of soul-stirring, light-gathering discoveries. With all that light oozing out of your pockets, no wonder you glow! But the greater mystery and delight isn't what's in *your* pocket, but that you have been in the Divine's pocket all long. How's *that* for a discovery?

Pull your discoveries out of your pocket. Write them next to mine, then speak them aloud. Speak them often. They are the truth of who you are:

7   I am One.

6   I trust.

5   I surrender.

4   I am open.

3   I am whole.

2   I am free.

1   I am ready.

Circle Back to the Beginning

How does one complete this soul vows journey through the chakras? I think the only answer is, one doesn't. There is no terminus. The sweet dance with your soul vows is not ending; it's really just beginning. Circle back to where you began when you felt the call to read this book and receive your soul vows. Your first discovery was "I am ready." Well, you are now ready to fully integrate your soul vows into your daily life. Pray them. Speak them. Chant them. Dance them. Feel them in your body. Plant them in your choices. Your soul vows will take it from here. They will teach you what they mean. Through them, and in them, and as them, you will become the living Presence of the Divine.

the dance of sacred unity

Our adventure began with a soft prelude beckoning you into an intimate dance with sacred unity. You heard your soul's deep desire to commit to values, and you answered. You felt the rhythm of what your soul knows—there is a Presence inside you. You memorized the words to your soul vows song by heart. You learned the steps to your very own gathering dance of Presence. This dance now belongs to you. You are the dance. As we end our sweet time together, and you twirl off to *be* the Beloved, listen to this one last chord of perfect harmony:

This
Union you want
With the earth and sky,
This union we all need with love,

A golden wing from God's heart just
Touched the ground,
Now
Step upon it
With your brave sun-vows
And help our eyes
To
Dance!

Hafiz, "This Union," from *The Gift*, translation by Daniel Ladinsky

the beloved and you are now one
in the dance of sacred unity.

isn't that divine?

resources

Masters and Mystics

Attar, Farid Ud-Din. *The Conference of the Birds* (Shambala Publications, 1971).

Douglas-Klotz, Neil. *Blessings of the Cosmos* (Sounds True, 2006).

Douglas-Klotz, Neil. *The Hidden Gospel* (Quest Books, 1999).

Douglas-Klotz, Neil. *The Sufi Book of Life* (Penguin Books, 2005).

Easwaran, Eknath, trans. *The Upanishads* (Nilgiri Press, 2007).

Fox, Matthew. *Breakthrough: Meister Eckhart's Creation Spirituality in New Translation* (Image, 1980). Republished by Inner Traditions in 2000 with the title *Passion for Creation: The Earth-Honoring Spirituality of Meister Eckhart*.

Hanh, Thich Nhat. *Living Buddha, Living Christ* (Riverhead Trade, Tenth Anniversary Edition, 2007).

Hanh, Thich Nhat. *You are Here* (Shambala Publications, 2009).

Khan, Pir Vilayat Inayat. *In Search of the Hidden Treasure* (Jeremy P. Tarcher/Penguin, 2003).

Neihardt, John G. *Black Elk Speaks* (University of Nebraska Press, 1972).

O'Neal, David, ed. *Meister Eckhart, from Whom God Hid Nothing* (New Seeds Books/Shambala, 1996).

Starr, Mirabai, trans. *The Showings of Julian of Norwich* (Hampton Roads, 2013).

Star, Jonathan, trans. *Tao Te Ching* (Jeremy P. Tarcher/Penguin, 2008).

Contemporary Spiritual Teachers

Bourgeault, Cynthia. *The Holy Trinity and the Law of Three* (Shambala Publications, 2013).

Helminski, Kabir. *Living Presence* (Jeremy P. Tarcher/Penguin, 1992).

Helminski, Kabir. *The Knowing Heart* (Shambala Publications, 1999).

Moore, Thomas. *Care of the Soul* (HarperCollins, 1992).

O'Donohue, John. *Anam Cara* (HarperCollins, 1997).

O'Donohue, John. *Beauty* (HarperCollins, 2004).

O'Donohue, John. *Eternal Echoes* (HarperCollins, 1999).

O'Donohue, John. *To Bless the Space Between Us* (Doubleday, 2008).

Rohr, Richard. *Immortal Diamond* (Jossey-Bass, 2013).

Rohr, Richard. *The Naked Now* (The Crossroad Publishing Company, 2009).

Starr, Mirabai. *God of Love* (Monkfish Book Publishing Company, 2012).

Vaughan-Lee, Llewellyn. *Fragments of a Love Story* (The Golden Sufi Center, 2011).

Spiritual Practice

Conner, Janet. *The Lotus and The Lily* (Conari Press, 2012).

Conner, Janet. *Writing Down Your Soul* (Conari Press, 2009).

Dreamer, Oriah Mountain. *The Dance* (HarperCollins, 2001).

Newberg, Andrew, and Mark Robert Waldman. *How God Changes Your Brain* (Ballantine Books, 2010).

Nouwen, Henri. *The Way of the Heart* (HarperOne, 2009).

Paintner, Christine Valters. *Lectio Divina: The Sacred Art: Transforming Words and Images into Heart-Centered Prayer* (SkyLight Paths, 2011).

Ryan, M. J., ed. *A Grateful Heart: Daily Blessings for the Evening Meal from Buddha to the Beatles* (Conari Press, 1994).

Shapiro, Rabbi Rami. *The Sacred Art of Lovingkindness: Preparing to Practice* (SkyLight Paths, 2006).

Steindl-Rast, David. *Gratefulness, the Heart of Prayer* (Paulist Press, 1984).

Thurman, Howard. *Meditations from the Heart* (Beacon Press, 1999).

Mystical Poetry

Barks, Coleman. *The Essential Rumi* (HarperOne, 2004).

Ladinsky, Daniel. *A Year with Hafiz* (Penguin, 2011).

Ladinsky, Daniel. *I Heard God Laughing* (Penguin, 2006).

Ladinsky, Daniel. *Love Poems from God* (Penguin, 2002).

Ladinsky, Daniel. *The Purity of Desire* (Penguin, 2012).

Ladinsky, Daniel. *The Gift* (Penguin, 1999).

Ladinsky, Daniel. *The Subject Tonight Is Love* (Penguin, 2003).

McNichols, William Hart, and Mirabai Starr. *Mother of God Similar to Fire* (Orbis Books, 2010).

Mitchell, Stephen. *The Enlightened Heart* (Harper Perennial, 1993).

Rilke, Rainer Maria. *Book of Hours: Love Poems to God*. Anita Barrows and Joanna Macy, trans. (Riverhead Books, 1996, 2005).

Whyte, David. *The House of Belonging* (Many Rivers Press, 1997).

Chakra System

Johari, Harish. *Chakras: Energy Centers of Transformation* (Destiny Books, 2000).

Judith, Anodea. *Wheels of Life: A User's Guide to the Chakra System* (Llewellyn Publications, 1987).

Myss, Caroline. *Anatomy of the Spirit: The Seven Stages of Power and Healing* (Harmony, 1997).

Music and Chant

Dances of Universal Peace, dancesofuniversalpeace.org

Gold, Rabbi Shefa. *The Magic of Hebrew Chant: Healing the Spirit, Transforming the Mind, Deepening Love* (Jewish Lights, 2013).

Hozeski, Bruce W., trans. *Hildegard of Bingen, The Book of the Rewards of Life.* (Oxford University Press, 1994).

Mathieu, W. A. *Bridge of Waves: What Music Is and How Listening to It Changes the World* (Shambala Publications, 2010).

Animal Wisdom

Andrews, Ted. *Animal Speak: The Spiritual & Magical Powers of Creatures Great and Small* (Llewellyn Publications, 2002).

Sams, Jamie, and David Carson. *Medicine Cards: The Discovery of Power Through the Ways of Animals* (St. Martin's Press, Revised Edition, 1999).

credits

your soul wants five things/your soul knows five things

Your Soul Wants Five Things is Janet Conner's signature series addressing the five essential longings of the soul. Janet offers the entire series or individual courses live each year. Writing Down Your Soul, Soul Vows, and The Lotus and The Lily are available from Conari Press. More at janetconner.com

Your Soul Wants	Your Soul Knows	Book and Course
1. to connect with Source	there is a **Voice** inside you	*Writing Down Your Soul*
2. to commit to values	there is a **Presence** inside you	*Soul Vows*
3. to serve a purpose	there is a **Purpose** inside you	*Soul Direction*
4. to express its beauty fully	there is a **Creator** inside you	*Plug In for Writers and Soul Expression*
5. to create life	there is a **Life** inside you	*The Lotus and The Lily*

about the author

Janet Conner is a writer, speaker, teacher, retreat guide, and radio show host with one compelling message: what you seek is inside. She is the author of Writing Down Your Soul and The Lotus and the Lily. She created The Soul-Directed Life radio show for Unity Online Radio. She lives and writes in Ozona, Florida, a tiny town on the Gulf of Mexico.

Visit her at www.janetconner.com.

to our readers

Conari Press, an imprint of Red Wheel/Weiser, publishes books on topics ranging from spirituality, personal growth, and relationships to women's issues, parenting, and social issues. Our mission is to publish quality books that will make a difference in people's lives—how we feel about ourselves and how we relate to one another. We value integrity, compassion, and receptivity, both in the books we publish and in the way we do business.

Our readers are our most important resource, and we appreciate your input, suggestions, and ideas about what you would like to see published.

Visit our website at www.redwheelweiser.com to learn about our upcoming books and free downloads, and be sure to go to www.redwheelweiser.com/newsletter to sign up for newsletters and exclusive offers.

You can also contact us at *info@rwwbooks.com.*

Conari Press
an imprint of Red Wheel/Weiser, LLC
665 Third Street, Suite 400
San Francisco, CA 94107